The Critical Idiom

Founder Editor: John D. Jump (1969–76)

37   The Short Story

In the same series

Tragedy *Clifford Leech*
Romanticism *Lillian R. Furst*
The Absurd *Arnold P. Hinchliffe*
Satire *Arthur Pollard*
Metre, Rhyme and Free Verse *G.S. Fraser*
Realism *Damian Grant*
The Romance *Gillian Beer*
Drama and the Dramatic *S.W. Dawson*
Plot *Elizabeth Dipple*
Irony and the Ironic *D.C. Muecke*
Allegory *John MacQueen*
Symbolism *Charles Chadwick*
The Epic *Paul Merchant*
Naturalism *Lilian R. Furst and Peter N. Skrine*
Rhetoric *Peter Dixon*
Comedy *Moelwyn Merchant*
Burlesque *John D. Jump*
The Grotesque *Philip Thomson*
Metaphor *Terence Hawkes*
The Sonnet *John Fuller*
The Ode *John D. Jump*
Myth *K.K. Ruthven*
Modern Verse Drama *Arnold P. Hinchliffe*
The Picaresque *Harry Sieber*
Biography *Alan Shelston*
The Stanza *Ernst Häublein*
Modernism *Peter Faulkner*
Dramatic Monologue *Alan Sinfield*
The Short Story *Ian Reid*
Comedy of Manners *David L. Hirst*
Farce *Jessica Milner Davis*
The Ballad *Alan Bold*
Genre *Heather Dubrow*
Tragicomedy *David L. Hirst*

The Short Story/

Ian Reid

Methuen

LONDON and NEW YORK

First published 1977 by
Methuen & Co. Ltd
11 New Fetter Lane, London EC4P 4EE
Reprinted twice
Reprinted 1984

Published in the USA by
Methuen & Co.
in association with Methuen, Inc.
733 Third Avenue, New York, NY 10017

© 1977 Ian Reid

Printed in Great Britain by
J. W. Arrowsmith Ltd, Bristol

ISBN 0 416 56060 1 (Hardback)
ISBN 0 416 56070 9 (Paperback)

For WENDY

(Ekki er langt um at gøra)

Contents

	Acknowledgements	ix
1	Problems of definition	1
	Critical neglect	1
	Protean variety	3
	When is a story not a story?	4
	How long is short?	9
	Translating terms	10
2	Growth of a genre	15
	From ancient to modern	15
	The Romantic impulse	27
3	Tributary forms	30
	Sketch	30
	Yarn	32
	Märchen	33
	Parable and fable	36
	Mixed modes	36
4	Brevity expanded	43
	Novella	43
	Cycle	46
	Framed miscellany	50
5	Essential qualities?	54
	'Unity of impression'	54
	'Moment of crisis'	55
	'Symmetry of design'	59
	Bibliography	67
	Index	73

Acknowledgements

It is difficult to know where a list of one's academic debts would begin or end. Several colleagues and students have contributed to the shaping of this monograph, and a roll-call of creditors is not the best way for me to thank them. But I do wish to record specifically my gratitude to the American Council of Learned Societies for awarding me a Fellowship which made possible some of the work drawn on here, to Professor Wolfgang Holdheim of the Comparative Literature Department at Cornell University for some helpfully long discussions of short fiction, and to Ms Robin Eaden for scrutinizing draft material.

I
Problems of definition

Critical neglect

Over the last 150 years the short story has come to figure conspicuously in the literature of several countries. Appearing in diverse periodicals as well as in books, it is probably the most widely read of all modern genres, and not only light-weight entertainers but also many distinguished fiction-writers during this period have found it congenial. Yet even now it seldom receives serious critical attention commensurate with that importance. Not until the OED Supplement of 1933 did the term 'short story' itself, designating a particular kind of literary product, gain formal admittance into the vocabulary of English readers. Theoretical discussion of the form had begun nearly a century before that tardy christening with some essays by Edgar Allan Poe, but was slow to develop and is still in an immature state. It seems to be impeded especially by problems connected with the popularity of the short-story genre.

Slightness and slickness, for instance, while not invariably resulting from brevity, do often infect the short story when it is adapting itself to market requirements. Magazine publication expanded hugely during the nineteenth century, tending to encourage stereotypes, mannerisms, gimmickry and the like. Consequently critics are sometimes reluctant to take the short story seriously as a substantial genre in its own right. Bernard Bergonzi, for one, thinks that 'the modern short-story writer is bound to see the world in a certain way' because the form he is using has an insidiously reductive effect: it is disposed 'to filter

down experience to the prime elements of defeat and aliena-
tion.' More satirically, Howard Nemerov applies these
belittling strictures:

> Short stories amount for the most part to parlor tricks, party
> favors with built-in snappers, gadgets for inducing recogni-
> tions and reversals: a small pump serves to build up the pres-
> sure, a tiny trigger releases it, there follows a puff and a flash
> as freedom and necessity combine; finally a celluloid doll
> drops from the muzzle and descends by parachute to the
> floor. These things happen, but they happen to no-one in par-
> ticular.

There are indeed many magazine stories that one could justly
dismiss in such terms, and it may well be true that even the
acme of short fiction hardly matches the greatest novels in
depicting the complex and wide-ranging nature of much
human experience. Complexity and breadth, however, are not
always the most central or interesting features of our lives.
Only a naive reader would confuse significance with bulk. The
lyric is by no means less potent and meaningful, inherently,
than a discursive poem, and the short story can move us by an
intensity which the novel is unable to sustain.

  Small-scale prose fiction deserves much more careful criticism, theoretical and practical, than it has usually had. It gets
elbowed out of curricula at the universities and elsewhere by its
heftier relatives, novel, poetry and drama; and of the countless
academic journals very few regularly give space to essays on
this neglected genre. Good books about the novel are legion;
good books about the short story are extremely scarce. Most
of those in English were written on the side by practitioners
such as H.E. Bates, Frank O'Connor and Sean O'Faolain. Germany has produced numerous scholarly studies of short fiction, but these are frequently impaired by a finicky taxonomic
purism which would set the *Novelle* in contradistinction to the
Kurzgeschichte, each regarded as a discrete type, whereas in

English usage 'short story' is an inclusive concept. The Russian school of formalist criticism, flourishing in the 1920s, generated sound work on theoretical aspects of the short story (notably essays by Boris Eichenbaum and Victor Shklovsky) and of its ancestor the *Märchen* (Vladimir Propp's classic account of 'The Morphology of the Folktale'), but permutations in the genre during the last half-century have outdated some of their findings. Those formalist investigations have recently been extended somewhat by the analytical 'narratology' of French structuralists such as Tzvetan Todorov and Claude Bremond, who however have not yet attended closely to any compositional principles which might be said to set the short story apart from the novel.

Protean variety
If on the one hand their popularity has tempted short stories towards the reductive formulae of merchandise, on the other hand it has sometimes encouraged protean variety. The taletelling impulse is too irrepressibly fecund to be confined within any single narrative pattern. Therefore the history of the modern short story embraces diverse tendencies, some of which have stretched, shrunk or otherwise altered previous conceptions of the nature of the genre. Ideas once proposed as definitive about the proper structure and subject material of the short story have needed revising to meet the facts of literary evolution. For example, nineteenth-century critics frequently insisted on the need for a firmly developed plot design in any 'true' short story; this was part of their effort to make the form respectable in terms of current taste, to lift it beyond its lowly origins. Some modern writers have undermined that principle of neat plot-making, both by bringing their fictions back in contact with various prototypical modes and by moving away from narrative techniques used in the novel towards the methods both of poetry (in their language, which is often more figurative and rhythmic than was usual in nineteenth-century

prose) and of drama (in their tendency to keep the narrator's voice out and rely on direct presentation of character and situation).

While it may be a sign of vigour, this variegated development is not conducive to establishing a precise descriptive vocabulary which would satisfy all critics. Yet if perfect consensus is lacking, adequate working definitions are nevertheless possible and helpful provided one recognizes that they must refer to predominant norms rather than all-inclusive categories, to evolving features rather than fixities and definites. At the risk of eroding completely any idea of an essential generic type, a quasi-Platonic form of the short story, we need to be empirically mindful of changes undergone by short prose fiction before and since its widespread acceptance in the Romantic period as a field of serious literary activity. If the New Testament parable, medieval French *fabliau*, seventeenth-century Chinese *p'ing-hua*, nineteenth-century American tall tale or recent experimental prose poem are to be regarded as outside the pale, they should still provide reference points for us in delimiting the territory of the short story proper. Accordingly the following chapters will examine some 'primitive' and proximate varieties of fiction, and look into the possibility that there may be certain formal properties which distinguish *the* short story ('Short-story', as Brander Matthews and others wanted to call it) from stories that just happen to be short.

When is a story not a story?

The simple term 'story' itself needs some preliminary attention. How strictly should one interpret it? Does it imply at least some plot, some sequence of narrated actions, or can a 'story' be purely descriptive in a static way?

E.M. Forster once represented himself as saying, in 'a sort of drooping regretful voice, "Yes - oh dear yes - the novel tells a story".' And the short story, we might think, can hardly justify its name if, on a smaller scale, it does not do likewise. Herbert

Gold, contributing to an 'International Symposium on the Short Story' in the *Kenyon Review* (XXX.4, 1968), asserts that 'the story-teller must have a story to tell, not merely some sweet prose to take out for a walk'. That seems reasonable as far as it goes. There remains, however, the fundamental question: what does 'story' mean? Few critics deign to examine such a rudimentary concept. We all know (it is ordinarily supposed) what a story is: a recital of events. But what constitutes an event? How many events go to make up a minimal story? Need they all be logically related to one another? Gerald Prince pursues these questions in his recent study *A Grammar of Stories,* using transformational principles derived from linguistics to account for the nature of tacit rules operating in various kinds of narrative. An event, he remarks, is a structural unit that can be summarized by a sentence of the simple kind which, in linguistic parlance, is the transform of less than two discrete elementary strings. Thus, 'Adam said that it was all Eve's fault' records a single event, whereas 'Adam blamed Eve, who had initially encouraged him to eat the apple' records two events, being derived from the transforms of two discrete elementary strings. At any rate, neither of these examples is a story in the proper sense. No story exists, says Prince, until three or more events are conjoined, with at least two of them occurring at different times and being causally linked. Other theorists have made similar observations: Claude Bremond, for instance, calls the requisite group of three events or stages of development *une séquence élémentaire.* 'Eve took a bite of the apple and then Adam did so too': that does not amount to even a skeletal story. But this does: 'Eve took a bite of the apple and then, at her urging, Adam did so too, as a result of which they became crazy and bit each other.' Temporal movement and logical linkage are just enough to make it a story, though no doubt insufficient to make it an interesting one.

We might ask in passing why a three-phase action is generally accepted as basic. Prince and others say nothing to explain this; it is adduced axiomatically, since it probably lies (though they do not admit as much) outside the scope of their strictly objective method, in the field of affective aesthetics. There may well be a connection here with Aristotle's sage remark, in the seventh chapter of his *Poetics,* that a plot must have beginning, middle and end in order to be a whole. And the same aesthetic pattern is evinced in that incremental trebling of actions which recurs in so many durably appealing tales. Our sense of shapeliness would not be satisfied if the poor woodcutter had only two magic wishes, or if four billy goats gruff crossed the troll's bridge, or if Goldilocks found five plates of porridge in the bears' cottage. (Indeed, in the latter story, there are not only three items in each bearish set but three sets too: only after the intruder has tried food, chairs and beds is it timely for the owners to return.) That there are seven dwarfs in Snow White's tale, that the valiant tailor kills seven flies with one blow - these and other numerical formulae are of a different sort, since they do not produce a structure of incremental narration. And besides, the point is not that a tripartite sequence is invariable in simple stories, just that its frequency seems to support the idea that a deep-rooted aesthetic preference is behind it.

We might also ask how important, or narrow, are the principles of temporal ordering and causal connectivity on which Prince insists. He is not alone in that insistence; most generalizations about the nature of narrative are to the same effect - and beg the same question. Arthur C. Danto, in his *Analytical Philosophy of History* (Cambridge, 1965), proposes that 'narratives are forms of explanation' (p. 233); accordingly, 'to tell a story is to exclude *some* happenings . . . . Stories, to be stories, must leave things out' (pp. 11-12). But how much can be left out? For Danto, 'explanation' means a delineated pattern of causation, and he expects this to involve a temporal process, a change of situation. Must every story be rationally coherent in those ways? Help with the problem could perhaps have been expected from the contemporary linguists who pursue under such various banners as discourse analysis or *Textgrammatik* or *translinguistique* the aim of distinguishing between a succession of sentences which are intelligibly connected and a succession of sentences which are randomly jumbled. But actually this kind of linguistic inquiry proves too inflexible to be applied usefully to literary narrative, which sometimes allows events to become unbonded while still retaining the reader's interest in the 'story'. Fiction can be as disjunctive, yet as emotionally compelling, as a weird dream; and not to let 'story' cover such cases would be to make the generic category more constricted than some modern story-tellers wish it to be. At a time when the border-lines of definition are in practice shifting outwards, an inclusive theoretical view has to be taken. To begin with, at least, let us regard almost any piece of brief fictional prose as a short story provided that, while it may lack a coherently sequential plot, it retains some clear formal relation to plotted stories. It may for instance present a surrealistic counterpart to any cause-and-effect organization of material, as in Sylvia Plath's 'Johnny Panic and the Bible of Dreams', Jan Gerhard Toonder's 'The Spider', or Franz Kafka's 'Ein Landarzt'. Or it may leave the reader to elicit a plot from disconnected data; Robert Coover's 'The Babysitter' offers a variety of alternative developments from the initial situation, each of these being a more or less credible fulfilment of fantasies in the minds of the characters. There is no defined story of an orthodox sort in 'The Babysitter', no single arrangement of happenings in whose actuality the author solicits our conventional belief. But psychological action is certainly there, and we may select a story from the available possibilities if we wish. More subversive still, yet parodically relevant to the tradition of plotted stories, is Jorge Luis Borges' 'El jardin de los senderos que se bifurcan' (The Garden of Forking Paths), which collapses normal distinctions between the veracious and the invented and which itself splits into several incompatible plot-paths so as to undermine the premise of causality on which narrative has usually depended. We can call these 'anti-stories' if we like, but that is implicitly to concede that they need to be seen in relation to the mainstream. Seemingly adversative developments often come to be absorbed within a generic tradition.

Having extended the concept 'short story' in certain respects, let us now venture some delimiting comments. For while narrowly prescriptive definitions will not do, since it is already clear that this genre has no monotypic purity, it would be useless to go to the latitudinarian extreme of including in it every kind of brief prose fiction. For instance, as Alfred G. Engstrom observes, 'legends of demons, saints, gods and the like and tales of outright wizardry' seldom have a claim to be considered short stories. They do not focus, as a rule, on human affairs and at any rate are not primarily intended as fictions. Thus we can discard the sort of thing recounted by Yeats in *The Celtic Twilight,* a scrapbook of local superstitions and spooky gossip, or material such as that collected by Martin Buber in *Tales of the Hasidim,* consisting largely of legendary anecdotes. But it is important to emphasize that what disqualifies such pieces is not the subject matter in itself, because that can give rise to admissible stories like Flaubert's 'La Légende de Saint Julien L'Hospitalier' which are shaped with artistry so as to convey a fully human dimension. The point is that unless there is something more than a fragmentary or an episodic structure, something more than a pious or a credulous tone, the potential interest of character in action will hardly be realized. This does not contradict the previous point that some apparently disjointed narratives may qualify as short stories. In particular instances it is usually easy to recognize sub-literary material by its lack of either formal poise or psychological cogency. *Exempla* about tediously saintly figures, snippets of legend about marvels and eerie occurrences: such things differ quite patently from those tales that are imaginatively cohesive even when fantastic and elliptical, or from tales that explore a mental and moral dimension by evoking the preternatural, as in Hawthorne's 'Young Goodman Brown' with its symbols of devilry and witchcraft.

How long is short?

With the kind of reservation just noted, one can say that in current usage 'short story' is generally applied to almost any kind of fictitious prose narrative briefer than a novel. This, however, needs further refining. What range of sizes does the term cover? How much contraction or protraction is allowable? Presumably the lower limit comes down in theory to a mere sentence, of the sort exemplified earlier, though in practice it is hard to imagine how anything under a page or two can offer more than a skinny outline of happenings (as with Hemingway's stringently abbreviated piece 'A Short Story') or a diminutive gesture towards some narrative possibilities (as with Fielding Dawson's 'Thunder Road'). The upper limit is less clear, and its demarcation will depend partly on whether author, reader or middleman is made the primary point of reference. Poe said that a 'tale' (which for the moment can be taken as a synonym; this and related designations will be discussed in later chapters) is capable of being perused at one sitting. The trouble with that idea, as William Saroyan once remarked, is that some people can sit for longer than others. Shifting the pragmatic focus, one may choose to let the matter of length be decided not by the reader's span of concentration so much as by editorial exigencies; Henry James mentions the 'hard-and-fast rule' among contemporary magazines of keeping inside the range of between six and eight thousand words. But of course such rules vary from time to time and magazine to magazine, so that a single piece of writing may fall within the bounds according to one editor yet be out of bounds according to another; generic lines need to be less arbitrarily drawn. An alternative possibility is to accept as short stories whatever an author wishes to nominate - or allows to be nominated - as such. Somerset Maugham notes in the preface to his *Complete Short Stories* that the smallest item there comes to about 1,600 words in all, the longest to about 20,000, and that is approximately the median range - though some authors would include briefer and longer work: in Frank Sargeson's *Collected Stories* a few pieces are less than 500 words, while one runs to about 32,000.

None of these alternatives seems wholly adequate. There is, however, no need to choose between them, because at any rate it would be unsatisfactory to make a word-count the sole criterion. Genre is not arithmetically defined. Aristotle could say that a tragic plot must have 'a certain magnitude', yet he made no attempt to measure that magnitude precisely; and while it can be said incontrovertibly that a short story must have a certain brevity, confining it within specific dimensions is futile. But if structural considerations, tectonic elements, are more important, they must nevertheless bear a relation to sheer size. That Sargeson story of 32,000 words, for instance, approaches in scale some other works of his which have been announced and accepted as 'novels'. What length can a short story reach without becoming a short novel? Is there indeed an intermediate category, as the increasingly frequent use in English criticism of the Italian word *novella* appears to suggest? This brings us up against another obstacle: the lack of a precise trans-lingual vocabulary for comparative purposes.

Translating terms

Generic definition becomes considerably more awkward once we extend the inquiry beyond literature and criticism in English. There is no exact equivalent to 'short story' in the usage of other European languages, only a cluster of like terms, most of which are confusingly cognate with the English word 'novel'. This difficulty needs clarifying historically. (The following paragraph is indebted to Gerald Gillespie's review of the terminological problem in *Neophilologus* for 1967.)

'Novel', from the sixteenth to the eighteenth centuries, had a meaning which, like the French *nouvelle,* stemmed from Italian *novella* and Spanish *novela;* it was applied, usually in the plural, to tales or short stories of the type contained in such works as Boccaccio's *Decameron,* the *Heptaméron* of Marguerite de Navarre, Cervantes' *Novelas Ejemplares* or Pettie's *Petite Pallace.* It referred to a fictitious prose narrative with characters or actions representing everyday life (sometimes in the past but more often in the present - hence 'new', a matter of novelty, a *novella*); and as such it stood in contrast to the traditional 'romance', which was less realistic and longer. As late as 1774 'novel' was still being regarded as a narrative of small compass: Chesterfield in his *Letters* described it as 'a kind of abbreviation of a Romance'. Only in the nineteenth century, when the old romance had declined further as a genre, did the concept of the novel expand to fill the space available. By then the word 'novel' had lost its original associations. But on the Continent its cognates, especially the German *Novelle,* continued to be linked in many writers' minds with the Renaissance *novella* despite an increasing disparity in size between much of their work and that small-scale prototype. In Boccaccio's hands the *novella* was very succinct, seldom extending to more than about ten pages. This was one of the ways in which it opposed the medieval romance, a diffuse form. But it did normally delineate a completed span of action (such as the full course of a love intrigue), and hence nineteenth-century writers could claim to be working within a tradition that stemmed from the *Decameron* even when their own narratives stretched to 150 pages. The process of expansion was in fact already under way in the *Novelas Ejemplares* (1613) of Cervantes, perhaps as important a progenitor as Boccaccio himself. A few critics, however, look sceptically at the idea of a tradition reaching from those earlier figures down into modern literature, and argue that the Italian term *novella* should not be applied to post-Renaissance forms; with works like Kleist's 'Michael

Kohlhaas' or Mérimée's 'Carmen' or Conrad's 'The Secret Sharer' or Lawrence's 'The Virgin and the Gipsy' we no longer have (these rigorists point out) the kind of economy, narrative frame, light tone, and so forth, that Boccaccio established. But that view is too fastidious. Every literary genre continually alters its shape, and due weight should be given to the fact that many writers did see themselves as belonging to a certain tradition.

In France a distinction between *nouvelle* and *conte* was available but not consistently observed. In 1664 La Fontaine entitled a collection of his verse tales (some of them derived from Boccaccio) *Nouvelles;* but a second series of the same works, issued the next year, was called *Contes et Nouvelles.* Even in the Romantic period these two terms were sometimes indiscriminately used, by de Musset and Nodier for instance, but around the mid-nineteenth century a distinction began to emerge: as Albert J. George observes in his study *Short Fiction in France, 1800-1850,* 'the word *conte* was assuming a meaning that differentiated it from *nouvelle,* the former accepted as more concentrated, with one major episode, the latter more complex and consisting of several scenes' (p. 234). *Conte,* like the English 'tale', implied a narrative manner reminiscent of oral delivery, and frequently contained an element of fantasy; a *nouvelle,* on the other hand, 'included a series of incidents for the analysis and development of character or motive' (George, p. 9), and - after Mérimée - tended towards an objective tone. But confusion remained; later in the century, works of this latter sort were often labelled *contes,* by Maupassant for instance.

In Germany, over that same period, classification was taken more seriously. Exactly what constituted a true *Novelle* was not a matter of complete agreement, but no-one doubted that it was a distinct and important genre. Various structural theories had their day, with Ludwig Tieck asserting that the action of a *Novelle* must have a 'curious, striking turning-point' (*son-*

derbaren, auffallenden Wendepunkt), Paul Heyse that it must have a quintessential silhouette, others that it must have a linear development, still others that it should follow a concentric path, and so forth. One fairly consistent tendency, however, among *Novelle* practitioners was to extend their compositions substantially. Consequently, when some German writers in recent times started to produce much more compressed stories, a different word had to be coined to distinguish these: *Kurzgeschichte*. This directly translates the English 'short story' - but its usage is narrowly confined to stories of a few pages only, whereas 'short story' is normally more flexible. Moreover, such had been the prestige of the *Novelle* that the *Kurzgeschichte* came to be regarded by some as an essentially inferior form: 'an illegitimate child of the *Novelle*', in Johannes Klein's words *(ein illegitimes Kind der Novelle)*. But even those German critics who do view the *Kurzgeschichte* without such prejudice have usually regarded it as something to be set in firm contradistinction to the *Novelle*. Thus Ruth J. Kilchenmann declares that the *Kurzgeschichte* presents 'a fragment of extracted experience' *(ein Stück herausgerissenes Leben)* while the *Novelle* is 'constructed around a crisis' *(auf einen Höhepunkt zu konstruiert);* that the plot of the *Kurzgeschichte* consists of 'netlike interweaving' *(netzhafte Verflechtung)* while that of the *Novelle* follows a 'rising and sharply falling curve' *(aufsteigende und scharf abfallende Kurve);* and that, in general, 'the compact, causally and logically built up form of the *Novelle* is in distinct contrast with the often desultorily, often arabesquely extended or concentrated and elliptical configuration of the *Kurzgeschichte*' *(Die dichte, kausal und logisch aufgebaute Form der Novelle hebt sich deutlich ab von der oft sprunghaften, oft arabeskenhaft erweiterten oder gerafften und aussparenden Gestaltung der Kurzgeschichte)*. This impressionistic scheme is attractive in its tidiness. Unfortunately short fiction, even in Germany, is too perversely untidy to conform to any such contrast.

What all this terminological flux indicates is a simple principle of literary evolution which was previously exemplified by the linked histories of the words 'novel' and 'romance'. As described by the Russian formalist Jurij Tynjanov half a century ago, this principle is based on the recognition that at any given time literature as a whole consists of a complex system of interrelated variable elements, including generic concepts. These concepts change as their context in the system changes. Thus, as we have seen, the scope of the 'novel' in eighteenth-century English literature became altered in direct proportion to a corresponding shift in the scope of the 'romance'. And similarly, 'short story' and *novella* are relative, even symbiotic, categories, sharing space as components in a total literary system which from time to time undergoes mutations:

> The size of a thing, the quantity of verbal material, is not an indifferent feature; we cannot, however, define the genre of a work if it is isolated from the system . . . . The study of isolated genres outside the features characteristic of the genre system with which they are related is impossible.

We shall need to return to the question whether the field of the short story is contiguous with that of the novel, or should be separated from it by an intermediate field. But these fields exist temporally as well as spatially, and in order to clarify our terms further we must now trace in broader outline the antecedents and emergence of what is usually meant by the 'modern short story'.

2
Growth of a genre

From ancient to modern

Observing where something has come from is not the same as defining what it has become. Nevertheless any generic definitions which aim to be precise and complete ought not to be formulated without a long historical perspective in mind. There is room in the present survey for only cursory reference to some early modes of short fiction, but that should be enough to indicate how variable this category is.

If asked to cite an antique example of a brief prose narrative many people would call to mind one of the memorable Old Testament stories, such as those concerning Joseph (Genesis xxxvii - xlvi), Samson (Judges xii - xvi) and Absalom (II Samuel xiii - xviii). These do have stylistic economy, psychological interest and so forth. Yet they are not offered as fictions; they purport to be historically veracious and to justify the ways of God to men. The same is even true of certain well-known passages of narrative in some of the Bible's apocryphal books: to us, the stories of Susannah and the elders or Bel and the Dragon, in which Daniel plays the role of a clever detective, are just that - stories; but they were not conceived as literary inventions, not shaped as contributions to the craft of fiction. So it is also with the New Testament parables, epitomic narratives which, though invented, are strictly governed by an explicit didactic purpose. We have to look beyond the Hebrew scriptures to ancient Egypt for the earliest extant stories, evidently told for their intrinsic value as entertainment. It is still possible to read with pleasure tales such as the Story of Sinuhe, or The Shipwrecked Sailor, which Egyptians wrote down early in the second millennium B.C.

Much the same as these in scope are numerous brief tales which appear in the classical and post-classical literature of Greece and Rome, often interpolated into larger works like the proto-novels of Petronius (the *Satyricon,* first century A.D.) and Apuleius *(Metamorphoses* or *The Golden Ass,* second century A.D.). (Needless to say, various other sorts of short fiction are to be found in Greek and Latin narrative writings, but these are usually in verse, as for instance in the case of the fables collected by Phaedrus and by Babrius in the first century A.D.; earlier Aesopic gatherings in prose, which do not survive, appear to have been designed for the rhetorical repertoire - rather like some modern Dictionary of Anecdotes for Public Speakers - and not as *belles lettres* in their own right.) Though placed within a larger context, prose tales of the sort included in the *Satyricon* have intrinsic artistic value. Here is a list of what typically constitutes one of these inset narratives:

> It is an imaginary story of limited length, intending to entertain, and describing an event in which the interest arises from the change in the fortunes of the leading characters or from behaviour characteristic of them; an event concerned with real-life people in a real-life setting.
>
> (Sophie Trenkner, *The Greek Novella in the Classical Period,* p. xiii)

When a narrative with those features had also an earthy, pungent quality it was known as 'Milesian', after one of the authors of them, Aristides of Miletus (*c.* 100 B.C.); collections of Milesian tales were made in Greece during the first two centuries B.C. and soon became popular in Latin translations also. Although these are not extant *in toto,* individual tales of the Milesian sort do survive in other works. An example is the neatly turned story of the Widow of Ephesus, related by Petro-nius, which goes as follows. A married woman of Ephesus, famous for her virtue, was so distraught when her husband died that she began a watch in his sepulchre, weeping incon-solably over the body. Several days and nights passed thus, dur-ing which this shining instance of fidelity became the talk of the town. Even the devoted maid who remained with the widow was unable to get her to eat, or to terminate this tearful vigil. Then it happened that some thieves were crucified nearby, a sol-dier being left on guard beside their crosses to prevent anyone from removing the bodies for burial. Hearing sounds of lamen-tation and seeing a light among the tombs, the soldier investi-gated. When he found there a woman of great beauty, sunk in grief, he fetched his supper and tried by various arguments to urge her to break her fast and desist from her profitless mourn-ing. She paid no attention, but her maid could not resist the proffered food and wine. Eventually, since the maid had yielded first, the widow allowed herself to be persuaded too. Further capitulation followed when the widow grew aware of the soldier's handsome appearance and fine manners. Undis-turbed by the corpse, they took their pleasure together in the tomb. Meanwhile, relatives of one of the crucified took his body away; and when the soldier discovered this he rushed back to the tomb and was about to kill himself - whereupon the virtuous widow stayed his hand: declaring she would rather see a dead man hung up than a living one struck down, she ordered that her late husband be affixed to the vacant cross. This was soon done, and all the living were happy ever after.

Not only has this story frequently been retold (by, among others, John of Salisbury in the twelfth century, La Fontaine in the seventeenth, Voltaire in the eighteenth and Christopher Fry in the twentieth), but it has a certain flavour, a piquancy of tone and plot, that we find in such latter-day writers as Maupas-sant. It smacks of the modern short story.

While some of this Hellenistic and Roman material trickled

through eventually into the reservoir of traditional story-telling from which authors have continued to draw, more important as source and stimulus over many centuries was a rich mass of oriental fiction. From medieval times onwards, several large, mobile tale-clusters infiltrated from Eastern cultures into European literature by various routes. There will be more to say in a later chapter about the form of these loose collections; for the present it is enough to describe them in broad outline. The most indefatigably migratory is the *Panchatantra*. In its original Sanskrit form it dates back at least to the early sixth century A.D.; in a variety of translations it spread through Europe in the Middle Ages; and Thomas North rendered it into English in 1570 - 'from an Italian version of a Latin version of a Hebrew version of an Arabic version of a (lost) Pahlavi [middle Iranian] version of some (lost) Sanskrit version of the original Panchatantra' (according to Franklin Edgerton, *The Panchatantra,* London, 1965, p.13). Similar to it in general shape, provenance and stamina, and even sharing with it a few individual tales, is a miscellany based on the story of Seven Sages whose narrative powers prevent a wrongly condemned prince from being executed. In Eastern versions it is a single philosopher who contrives the stay of execution, not a group of seven wise men, and his name gives those versions their usual title, *The Book of Sindibad.* Belonging to that same family of popular books is *The Book of the Wiles of Women,* a form of *Sindibad* which reached Europe in the thirteenth century and enjoyed a widespread vogue by affecting a moral purpose. (In contrast, the *Thousand and One Nights* had no need to disguise its fantasies as *exempla* for readers in the West, for although it began to take shape in Persia by the tenth century and was current in Egypt by the twelfth, it did not find a European translator until the eighteenth; its array of *contes arabes,* as the subtitle designated them, could then be enjoyed frankly for their exotic and erotic appeal.)

Apart from dull devotional and instructive pieces, it was not common in the medieval period for short narratives to be written in prose. Heroic episodes such as the *Battle of Maldon* are in verse; the *fabliaux,* low-life comic tales of French origin such as the one told by Chaucer's Miller, are in verse; the Breton *lais,* popularized by the Norman writer Marie de France and represented in English by works like the fourteenth-century *Sir Launfal,* are in verse. When prose is the medium, the usual result is tedium: heavy homiletic considerations dominate, regardless of artistry. There are partial exceptions in Old Norse literature. The *Prose Edda* of Snorri Sturluson, written in Iceland in the early thirteenth century, contains some fine myths and legends, succinctly told. But these are part of a treatise on the art of skaldic (courtly) verse of the Viking era. *Edda* means something like 'poetics'; Snorri's primary purpose is to compile a handbook on matters of metrics, diction and style, and the narratives for which we now chiefly prize it he includes merely by way of an introductory survey of ancient Scandinavian mythology and heroic stories. The prose parts subserve the supposedly higher art of poetry. A few of the Icelandic sagas are fairly brief, but though terse in expression they are more like novels than short stories in scope, usually chronicling an extensive series of events. This is true, for instance, of *Hrafnkels saga,* one of the shortest, which runs to about 9,000 words. Nearer to the short story are the *þættir,* episodes set into longer works like *Morkinskinna,* a compendious history of Norwegian kings.

In southern Europe, the work which established prose as an attractive option for the literary artist was Boccaccio's *Decameron* (finished in the 1350s). Erich Auerbach, in chapter 9 of his masterly critical study *Mimesis* (1946; English translation by Willard R. Trask, 1953), shows through detailed stylistic analysis how Boccaccio enriches the vernacular by subtle rhetorical treatment, without losing the tone and tempo of oral narration, to produce a language more resourceful than anything used by his medieval predecessors. At the same time Boccaccio freed fiction from the dead hand of didacticism by blending courtly romance elements with low *fabliau* material and by playfully modifying certain pious medieval forms, such as the saint's legend, parodied in I,1 and III,10, and the *exemplum,* drawn on in IV,2. This latter tale will serve to illustrate the way in which Boccaccio's stylistic achievement involves structural refinement and a tone of genial wit. Pampinea, who narrates the story of IV,2, introduces it with reference to the proverbial truism that a wolf can soon have its way by donning sheep's clothing. The ensuing narrative, says Pampinea, will exemplify this (morally dubious) proposition. But in fact it does not do so, ultimately; though initially successful, the rogue is brought low in the final outcome. Yet the tone in which this outcome is related is far from being that of a sober sermonic *exemplum.* The 'justice' served out to Friar Alberto is less moral than poetic. This comes about through a second twist to the process whereby he has turned someone's folly to his own account. Alberto, a lecherous fellow masquerading as a Friar, discovers through his role as confessor that a certain scatter-brained young woman, Lisetta, has a ludicrously conceited estimation of her charms: her beauty, she declares, 'would be deemed remarkable even in Heaven itself'. Alberto makes a pretence of rebuking her sternly for her vanity, but later visits her with the story that he has been severely chastized for his insolence by none other than the Angel Gabriel, who instructed him to seek forgiveness at once from Lisetta; her beauty is indeed heavenly, Gabriel has told him, and moreover Gabriel admires her so much that he wants to spend a night with her - in human form, for convenience. Lisetta is enraptured, and agrees to Alberto's request that she should pray to Gabriel to use Alberto's body for the purpose, since while the Friar's body is angelically occupied his soul will be temporarily in Heaven. All goes according to plan: Lisetta's husband being abroad, Alberto/ Gabriel is able to pay regular nocturnal visits to her bedroom, where he 'flies without wings'. But Lisetta cannot resist boasting to an acquaintance that she has celestial connections of an intimate sort, and before long all Venice knows of her gullibility. Her brother-in-laws, hearing the news, resolve to track down this angel and 'see whether he can fly'. When they hammer at her door, Alberto jumps from the bed, takes 'a flying leap' through the window into the canal, swims to the other side, and begs an honest-looking man there to shelter him, spinning a yarn to explain his nude condition. The man agrees, in return for some money which Alberto arranges to have paid to him, and hides the Friar in his house. After hearing from the town gossips how Lisetta's in-laws had entered her house to find that 'Gabriel had flown, leaving his wings behind him', the man guesses whom he is harbouring. He tells Alberto that, since the in-laws are searching the city for him, his only chance of escaping undetected is by disguising himself and joining a fancy-dress carnival due to take place that very day in St Mark's Square, then slipping away from the crowd afterwards. Alberto allows himself to be dressed as a masked savage, smeared with honey and feathers, and sets out with the honest fellow - who, however, has secretly sent word ahead that the Angel Gabriel will soon be on display in St Mark's Square. And there the wretched Alberto is unmasked and subjected to public ridicule and abuse. What gives this story shape is not any crudely moralistic point but the comic play on metaphorically linked transformations. Having exploited the credulous literalism of Lisetta's flights of vain fancy in order to make his amorous flights, Alberto finds his own imposture literalized in the ironic denouement of the story: he must fly from his pursuers, seeming to elude them only to acquire the feathers not of an angelic creature but of a sub-human one.

Boccaccio's influence on Renaissance narrative was as various as it was palpable. In France, Marguerite de Navarre's *Heptaméron* (1558) borrowed the structural formula by which Boccaccio linked and framed his tales. In England, though no translation of *The Decameron* in its entirety appeared until

1620, there were three collections of *novelle*, largely derived from the Italian and French models, in 1566-76: William Painter's *Palace of Pleasure*, Geoffrey Fenton's *Certain Tragical Discourses*, and George Pettie's *A Petite Pallace of Pettie his Pleasure*. In Spain, Cervantes' *Novelas Ejemplares* (1613) combined Boccaccio's anecdotal liveliness and interest in psychological motivation with a new dimension of moral seriousness. While not 'exemplary' in any narrow didactic sense, the Cervantine *novela* evinces a keen interest in problems of behaviour. In 'The Jealous Extramaduran', for instance, the husband's jealousy is not (as it is typically in *fabliaux*) an excuse for his wife's infidelity, but the story's epicentre, a symptom of insecurity more basic than sex.

For about two centuries after Cervantes there were few developments in European fiction worth noting here. Individual writers like Diderot did keep alive the narrative possibilities which Boccaccio, Cervantes and others had broached so vigorously. But the eighteenth century generally was not notable for any sustained or adventurous exploration of the 'new' form, the *novella* or short story. Some writers toyed with the oriental tale; it was used occasionally, for example, by Addison and Steele as a kind of decorative appendage to essays in *The Spectator*, and by Voltaire for light satire in *Zadig*. The 'character', a fictional portrait-essay sketching a representative personality-type in the manner of Theophrastus and La Bruyère, also enjoyed some currency in the periodicals, but gave no scope for either psychological complexity or plot interest. After the Renaissance *novella*, the next upsurge of short fiction came as part of the swelling tide of Romanticism. Germany, France, Russia and America saw the most energetic initiatives.

In Germany the *Novelle* quickly became during the early nineteenth century a highly developed literary form, taken up by numerous talented authors and subjected to serious theorizing. Its complex evolution has been thoroughly charted by Johannes Klein in *Geschichte der Deutschen Novelle*, by E.K.

Bennett and H.M. Waidson in *A History of the German Novelle,* and by others. A point worth emphasis, however, is that the emerging *Novelle* was not the only kind of short prose fiction to attract German writers of the Romantic period. This was, after all, a time of interest in German folk-lore, as two famous collections testify: *Des Knaben Wunderhorn* (1805-8), consisting of songs gathered by Achim von Arnim and Clemens Brentano, and the *Kinder- und Hausmärchen* (Childhood and Household Tales) assembled by the brothers Grimm (1812-23). The same interfusion of natural and supernatural, mundane and marvellous, which occurs in this folk material was conjured up also in numerous *Kunstmärchen* ('Art' Tales) composed by sophisticated writers like Tieck, Brentano and Hoffmann. The *Novelle,* it is often said, presents events as being logically and causally interconnected; very often the *Kunstmärchen,* on the other hand, indicates no rationally explicable motivation for the actions and situations it depicts. Works such as Tieck's 'Der blonde Eckbert' (Blond Eckbert, 1797) or Hoffmann's 'Der goldne Topf' (The Golden Pot, 1814) evoke a sense of the mysterious within the field of everyday reality. Strange encounters and metamorphoses may happen - or seem to happen: nothing is objectively verifiable - anywhere, at any time, in a Dresden cafe as well as down some country byway. A full-length study of the *Kunstmärchen* available to English readers is Marianne Thalmann's *The Romantic Fairy Tale: Seeds of Surrealism,* translated by Mary B. Corcoran. Something of the impulse behind the *Märchen* entered the *Novelle,* and the two forms are less clearly distinguishable than theorists sometimes suggest. Even the austere *Novellen* of Heinrich von Kleist, for instance, implicitly subvert the notion that events always follow a rational pattern. Not until mid-century, with the work of Stifter, Keller, Storm and others, did German narrative prose turn into more soberly realistic channels.

In France the art of the short story was firmly established in

1829-31 with the magazine publication of a dozen *contes* by Mérimée, Balzac and Gautier, though the substantial developments came much later: the pastoral freshness of Daudet's *Lettres de Mon Moulin* (1869), the cool, meticulous objectivity of Flaubert's *Trois Contes* (1877), and the more styptic naturalism of Maupassant's prolific output in the 1880s. Not the least important tendency of those latter writers was their predilection for rural subjects and simple folk. Mostly it could be left to the novel to delineate those large-scale social patterns which were so amply extended in urban life; the short story seemed especially suitable for the portrayal of regional life, or of individuals who, though situated in a city, lived there as aliens.

Something similar emerged also in Russia, where, after Pushkin had initiated imaginative work in short prose fiction, Gogol and Turgenev gave it a particular direction. Pushkin's *Tales of Bjelkin* (1830) brought bareness and concision into Russian literature; in pieces like 'The Shot', all padding is removed and an interest in narrative perspective becomes central. But Pushkin's fictive world is still an aristocratic one, whereas what makes Gogol notable is not just that he was intent, even more than Pushkin, on stripping narrative prose of fuzzy embellishment, but also that he wrote of ordinary people, apparent nonentities, with an attentiveness capable of revealing deep currents of emotion beneath petty surfaces. The details of peasant life in the Ukraine or of the pathetic tribulations of a copying clerk in Petersburg could be, he showed, as compelling as any intrigues of the salon or gaming table. 'He took the short story some way back to the folk-tale', remarks H.E. Bates in *The Modern Short Story*, 'and in doing so bound it to earth.' Gogol's stories appeared in the decade up to 1842, when the most influential of them, 'The Overcoat', was published. Its seminal importance for later writers was acknowledged by Turgenev: 'We have all come out from under Gogol's "Overcoat".' Turgenev's own volume, *A Sportsman's Sketches* (1846), augments the efforts of Gogol, both in its way of compacting into a few casual phrases the essence of a person's experience and in its focusing on society's misfits and underdogs - in this case the Russian serfs.

Of nineteenth-century English-language writers it was not the British, preoccupied with the expansive novel, who turned to the short story, but the Americans. Even in America it took some time for this form to be clearly identified. Fred Lewis Pattee, in his historical survey *The Development of the American Short Story,* points out that the term 'short story' itself, used generically to designate an independent literary form rather than just a story that lacks length, is as recent as the 1880s. Washington Irving, author of 'Rip Van Winkle' and 'The Legend of Sleepy Hollow', called his writings 'sketches' or 'tales', and the latter term was preferred by Poe, Hawthorne and Melville. Indeed, 'tale' is apt for the kind of fiction these writers were mostly producing in the '30s and '40s, with its stylized characterization, detachment from normal social behaviour, and tendency towards allegory. While their work undoubtedly has a prominent place within the comprehensive history of the short story, it is distinguishable from what some critics regard as the short story proper, a more 'realistic' sort. In a recent article, 'From Tale to Short Story: The Emergence of a New Genre in the 1850s', Robert F. Marler traces the decay of the tale after mid-century by examining American magazine fiction in which 'the comparatively balanced effects of Irving's sentimentalism, Poe's sensationalism, and Hawthorne's moralism were . . . heavily emphasized, distorted, and unconsciously parodied'. These excesses led to a reaction during the 'fifties. Surveying critical commentary in periodicals of that decade, Marler detects 'dissatisfaction with the conventional tale' and the growth of 'opinion that was congenial to the development of the short story.' Although no explicit classification was made at the time, a separation of the two kinds of narrative was in process. This background, Marler argues cogently, is reflected in the increasing advocacy of realism, of depicting ordinary experience plausibly, of keeping 'vividly true to daguerrotype-like studies of life', as one magazine editor put it in 1858. (The excitement resulting from the invention of photography was still very strong then, and no doubt partly explains the increasing prestige of realism in art.) Stories began to emerge which aimed at an impression of actuality: regionalist vignettes, for example, and fiction of such psychological subtlety as Melville's 'Bartleby the Scrivener' (in contrast to the same author's romantic tales, like 'The Bell-Tower'), and humorous yarns. Folk humour was especially important in registering and reinforcing the shift in public taste away from distended tales towards realistic stories. Popular Southwestern humour gained access to literary magazines in the East at about that time, and even in its most extreme forms (so-called 'tall tales', where 'tale' denotes consciously ludicrous distortion) this was usually characterized by a kind of irony and authenticity which ran counter to the emotive inflation of the decadent kind of tale. Marler makes this observation:

> The tall tale, having received the East's stamp of approval, was a force for realism because the colloquial teller (as opposed to the narrator in the frame) was often convincing as a personality and because many such narratives relinquished their humour for the serious treatment of human foibles.

One of the most successful writers of that period was Bret Harte, author of 'The Luck of Roaring Camp' and other local-colour stories of the Californian goldfields. Looking back later at the development of American fiction during his time, Harte remarked that the most important formative influence on it was humour:

> Crude at first, it received a literary polish in the press, but its dominant quality remained. It was concise and condensed, yet suggestive. It was delightfully extravagant, or a miracle

of understatement . . . . It gave a new interest to slang . . . . It
was the parent of the American short story.
(Quoted by H.E. Bates, *The Modern Short Story,* p.49)

In this context, 'humour' includes not only what is seen as
amusing but also what is seen as wry, poignant, disillusioned.
Constance Rourke's excellent book, *American Humor* (New
York, 1933) traces this varied nineteenth-century comic tradition with particular reference to three central figures of American folk-lore: the shrewd itinerant Yankee pedlar, the
audacious roving backwoods frontiersman, and the resilient
displaced Negro slave. Why these character-types and the
strand of native humour they represent found expression
chiefly in the short story form is a question that Rourke does
not consider; but part of the answer presumably lies in the fact
that each of those three figures is a wanderer, and whereas the
conventional nineteenth-century novel normally accommo-
dates the processes of a dense, ordered society, the short story
has been, in Frank O'Connor's words, 'by its very nature re-
mote from the community - romantic, individualistic, and
intransigent' *(The Lonely Voice,* p.21).

The Romantic impulse
O'Connor's observation is suggestive. Short stories do frequently focus on one or two individuals who are seen as separp-
ated from their fellow-men in some way, at odds with social
norms, beyond the pale. In this respect short stories can
properly be called romantic, as O'Connor proposes, or even
Romantic by virtue of their affinity with those works by Wordsworth, Coleridge, Byron, Nerval and others through which
move wanderers, lonely dreamers, and outcast or scapegoat
figures. Indeed, since the emergence of the short story as a fully
fledged genre in Europe and America coincides, as already
noted, with the burgeoning of that protean cultural pheno-
menon known as Romanticism, there would seem to be a

broad basis for the common remark that the short story is in essence a Romantic form: *the* Romantic prose form. In its normally limited scope and subjective orientation it corresponds to the lyric poem as the novel does to the epic. That the brief, personally expressive lyric is the paramount kind of Romantic poem, in contrast to the predominantly discursive modes of Augustan verse, is a point that needs no emphasis; and its brevity was often regarded as its primary quality. Poe's essays go as far as to assert, repeatedly, that the 'degree of excitement which would entitle a poem to be so called at all cannot be sustained throughout a composition of any great length'; and by the same token, he argues, a short prose narrative which can be read at one sitting is *ipso facto* superior to any novel. That view is extreme, but there is more plausibility in the related point that the short story, like much characteristically Romantic poetry, tends to concentrate on some significant moment, some instant of perception. Just as Wordsworth records in *The Prelude* certain 'spots of time', and Keats celebrates in his Odes the intense sensation or insight that transcends time, so one could say that the short story typically centres on the inward meaning of a crucial event, on sudden momentous intuitions, 'epiphanies' in James Joyce's sense of that word; by virtue of its brevity and delicacy it can, for example, single out with special precision those occasions when an individual is most alert or most alone.

That the thrust of Romanticism was one of the main forces propelling the nineteenth-century short story into the salient position it came to occupy is undeniable, as is the fact that the genre has continued in the main to exhibit 'Romantic' attitudes of the kind just mentioned. A few reservations should be noted, however, because its development cannot be explained solely and sufficiently in a context of literary culture. Even a superficial comparison of English and American literature, for example, makes that very clear: English writers were affected quite as much as Americans by the Romantic impulse, yet their output of short fiction during the nineteenth century was virtually negligible. Two broad explanations have been adduced to account for this, one in terms of social structures and one in terms of the magazine market. In the first place it is pointed out that, unlike the novel, which was urban, urbane and bourgeois in its origins and which was concerned chiefly with manners, marriage and money, the short story found its province more often than not among small groups of working men, especially in those many areas of the American continent which by the early nineteenth century had come to consist of regional settlements still lacking social cohesion. As for the market factor, it issued chiefly from the absence of international copyright regulations and the consequent proliferation in America of cheap reprints from overseas. Since British novels could be pirated so simply and profitably, American publishers were seldom keen to sponsor work by local novelists, a costly luxury. The short story, on the other hand, could find a ready public through the gift annuals and periodicals, which became increasingly popular after about 1830. Among those whose fiction appeared in these 'slicks' were such eminent writers as Poe and Hawthorne.

One further reservation needs to be attached to any description of the short story as an essentially Romantic form: while it may be true that in its nineteenth-century development the short story normally incorporated such Romantic features as the singling out of a significant moment of awareness, it does not follow that any such features are essential to the genre. We shall pursue this point in the final chapter.

3
Tributary forms

Some narrative categories mentioned so far need sorting out now more analytically. Quite separate in their historical derivations and in some latter-day revivals, these almost amount to distinct genres in themselves. Of course, their distinctness is not always preserved; as we shall see later in this chapter, two or more traditional currents often converge during one story, so that a reader's attention may have to keep refocusing as the various conventions flow together. But first, the main tributaries can be singled out here.

Sketch

There is a broad initial distinction between writing about *conditions* and writing about *events*. On the one hand primary emphasis falls on what some thing, place or person is like; on the other, it falls on what happens. The former, then, is predominantly descriptive, while the latter follows a line of action. The way they differ is analogous to the contrast between sentences whose subject is depicted by an adjectival predicate ('Fred was an unhappy chap with a fixed scowl on his face . . . ') and sentences whose subject is enacted by verbs ('Once upon a time a damsel set off to seek her fortune . . . '). The first of these is a sketch; the second, having an anecdotal core, usually develops into a tale, and more particularly into a yarn.

The sketch proper is virtually static. Washington Irving, one of its chief exponents, gives us a working definition. Although the most durable pieces in his *Sketch Book* (1820) were actually yarns like 'Rip Van Winkle' and 'The Legend of Sleepy Hollow', the majority (in accordance with the book's title) contain these elements, which Irving said he wanted mainly to convey: 'The play of thought, and sentiments and language; the weaving in of characters, lightly yet expressively delineated; the familiar and faithful exhibition of scenes in common life; and the half-concealed vein of humor that is often playing through the whole.' Several other American writers in the 1820s and early '30s produced sketches, especially regional vignettes of local scenery, customs and the like. At about the same time in England something similar is to be found in the work of essayists. Charles Lamb occasionally introduces a sketch into some of his writings; the main purpose of 'South Sea House' and 'Oxford in the Vacation' is to limn a scene in the memory. A few decades later, Walter Pater's interest in personality (of the contemplative rather than active cast) expresses itself in 'The Child in the House' and other such 'imaginary portraits', as he called them. More recently still, George Orwell's famous essay 'Shooting an Elephant' approximates to a sketch, concentrating descriptively as it does on the outlines of one situation. Eighteenth-century periodical writers, too, had produced sketch-like pieces when depicting fictitious personages (most memorably, 'Sir Roger de Coverley' in the *Spectator* essays of Addison and Steele) without involving them in any chain of substantial events. On the other hand the seventeenth-century 'character' and its Theophrastan prototype differ from the sketch because they present not specific individuals but abstract human categories, like Joseph Hall's 'The Malcontent' ('Everie thing he medleth with, hee either findeth imperfect, or maketh so: neither is there anie thing that soundeth so harsh in his eare as the commendation of another ... '), or Thomas Overbury's 'A Puritan' ('Where the gate stands open, he is ever seeking a stile: and where his Learning ought to climbe, he creepes through ... '), or Jean de La Bruyère's 'A Coquette' ('. . . never succumbs to her passion for pleasing, nor to the high opinion she holds of her own beauty; she regards time and years only as things that wrinkle and disfigure other women, forgetting that age is written on her face . . . ').

While the mere landscape-essay or pen-portrait can hardly be called a short story, there is usually in the sketch some movement towards a narrative dimension. Examples of stories that are predominantly sketches range from character studies like Joyce's 'Clay', Thurber's 'Doc Marlow', Mann's 'The Infant Prodigy' and several of Mansfield's 'German Pension' pieces to Walser's many atmospheric *Skizze* describing walks and encounters in Switzerland and Lawson's evocations of aspects of the Australian bush ('In a Dry Season', 'In a Wet Season').

Yarn

Just as the simplest kind of plotless sketch is too deficient in human action and motivation to be regarded as a true short story, so too is the mere anecdote, which recounts a single fragmentary episode (often about something supposed to have happened to a well-known person: George Washington and the felling of the cherry tree, Isaac Newton and the falling of the apple, King Alfred and the burning of the cakes). Anecdotes are by no means all structurally identical; they may take several of the rudimentary literary shapes posited by André Jolles in his *Einfache Formen* (1930), such as the local legend (German *Sage* - the Pied Piper of Hamelin, for instance), or joke *(Witz);* they may be attached to a proverb *(Spruch)* or riddle *(Ratsel)*. But anecdotes verge on the modern short story only when amplified as tales.

The term 'tale' has often been applied to almost any kind of narrative, whether of fictitious or actual events, and remains too imprecise to be of much use for discriminative purposes. But usually it designates a fairly straightforward, loose-knit account of strange happenings. Among the several specific sorts of tales are the gest (from Latin *gesta,* deeds), relating adventurous exploits; the ballad, a versified or sung tale in a

popular and often romantic vein; the fairy-story, to be discussed presently; and the yarn.

An elaborated anecdote or series of anecdotes, the yarn is
narrated in colloquial and the casual tones appropriate to a rac-
onteur working in oral tradition. The word derives from sail-
ors' slang in which rope-making became a metaphor for story-
spinning, and 'yarn' still usually implies the atmosphere of the
foc's'le (or bar-room, campfire, club-house or the like). The
implicit norm is naturalistic (unlike that of fairy-stories, which
have a preternatural orientation). This holds true even for the
extravagant sort of yarn known as the tall tale; while its
material may be highly improbable, it is related in a matter-of-
fact-way. Perhaps the best-known exemplar of the yarn is
Mark Twain. Such features as the vernacular idiom, the
broadly comic tendency, the paratactic structure, and the
emphasis on externals rather than psychological factors are to
be found for instance in that often anthologized piece by
Twain, 'The Celebrated Jumping Frog of Calaveras County'.
More recently, the primitive American tall tale was revived in
Stephen Vincent Benet's 'The Devil and Daniel Webster'.

While innumerable yarns issued from the American fron-
tier, the Australian outback, and similar areas of fringe settle-
ment elsewhere, closely comparable forms did develop also in
some established cultures. Examples are the Chinese *p'ing hua*
and Russian *skaz*. The former, flourishing in the early seventeenth century, was essentially a popular tale dominated by its
narrator's presence and colloquial idiom; frequently fantastic
in content, it was nevertheless always realistic in tone. The *skaz*
is a kind of dramatic monologue in which the narrator's habits
of speech contribute importantly to the effect of what he
relates.

Märchen

Whereas the yarn and its close cousins stem from the kind of
folk-tale in which everyday life is an implied touchstone, the

fairy-story is the kind which appeals to our sense of the marvellous. We suspend disbelief and allow patterns of wish-fulfilment to have free reign. J.R.R. Tolkien describes its proper subject as follows:

> Fairy-stories are not in normal English usage stories *about* fairies or elves, but stories about Fairy, that is *Faerie,* the realm or state in which fairies have their being. *Faerie* contains many things besides elves and fays, and besides dwarfs, witches, trolls, giants, or dragons: it holds the seas, the sun, the moon, the sky; and the earth, . . . and ourselves, mortal men, when we are enchanted . . . .

> A 'fairy-story' is one which touches on or uses Faerie, whatever its own main purpose may be: satire, adventure, morality, fantasy. Faerie itself may perhaps most nearly be translated by Magic - but it is magic of a peculiar mood and power, at the furthest pole from the vulgar devices of the laborious, scientific, magician.

Since, however, the connotations of 'fairy-story' have become debased by association with those dimunitive tinselled creatures that plague second-rate books for children, the German word *Märchen* is often used instead in the English critical lexicon.

We have already noted, in chapter 2, that many such tales found their way into the mainstream of German literature during the early nineteenth century, both from genuine folk material (in the famous Grimm collection) and as *Kunstmärchen* composed by Hoffman and others. These two sorts of *Märchen* - primary and secondary, anonymous oral tradition and conscious artistic adaptation - are of course to be found also in other countries. In France, more than a century before the Grimms, Charles Perrault gathered his *Contes de ma Mère l'Oye,* which include such familiar items as 'Puss-in-Boots', 'Little Red Riding Hood', 'Cinderella' and 'The Sleeping

Beauty'. Though smoothly polished by Perrault, these remain close to the simple contours of orally transmitted narratives, *le merveilleux traditionnel*. About 1830, under the influence of Hoffmann, French writers such as Nodier and Nerval began to produce what became known as the *conte fantastique,* having some of the features of folk-tales but being characterized, as P.-G. Castex remarks,

> par une intrusion brutale du mystère dans le cadre de la vie réelle; il est généralement lié aux états morbides de la conscience . . .

> (by a brutal intrusion of mystery into the compass of everyday life; it is generally linked with the morbid states of consciousness . . .)

Irish literature, too, abounds in vigorous examples not only of traditional stories of the *Märchen* type (the Gaelic *seansgéal)* but also of individual compositions by writers like George Moore which try to recreate something of the same oral quality. Vivian Mercier gives a thorough account of that subject in his article 'The Irish Short Story and Oral Tradition'.

Since supernatural elements figure conspicuously in the *Märchen,* how does it differ from the myth? Anthropologists from Franz Boas and Ruth Benedict to Claude Lévi-Strauss have taken the view that myths and folk-tales share much the same kind of content, interchanging their themes and motifs so often that there can be no absolute distinction between the two categories. In fact, however, they are quite separable in two important respects. First, their preoccupations differ markedly - on the one hand religious matters, aristocratic heroism, and so forth; on the other, the familiar daydreams and nightmares of ordinary folk. Moreover, whereas myth is manifold and diversiform, the *Märchen* shapes its material (whether derived from mythology or not) according to a particular kind of limited formal pattern. This pattern was demonstrated strikingly in a study made by the Russian formalist Vladimir Propp in 1928 and translated into English thirty years later as *Morphology of the Folk-Tale*. Propp's discovery, after analysing the structure of a hundred Russian fairy-stories, was that although particular elements (such as character attributes) vary from story to story their basic functions in the plot are rigorously limited and conform to a regular sequence. Thus the villainous character may be (e.g.) a witch or a dragon or an ogre, the hero's initial misfortune may involve (e.g.) a material deficiency or an inflicted injury, and so on; but the maximum number of roles never exceeds seven (hero, princess, provider, etc.) and the maximum number of units of action (hero leaves home, hero acquires magical help, villain is punished, etc.) never exceeds thirty-one. No tale has all thirty-one functions, but such of them as each tale does have will always follow a constant order.

Propp's emphasis on the strict interrelations of narrative components has become very influential in recent years. Several critics, most notably the French structuralists A.J. Greimas, Claude Bremond and Tzvetan Todorov, have tried to develop his insight into a more general theory of fiction. Their interest, however, focuses more on the nature of narration itself than on generic concepts, and so far they have had little to say about the short story specifically.

Parable and fable

The parable and fable were closely akin in their simple premodern forms, each being shaped towards a conspicuous analogy between the main narrative elements and certain aspects of general human behaviour. In addition to the most obvious difference, that the fable endows animals (or sometimes vegetable and mineral objects) with human capabilities, there are other ways in which the two forms are distinguishable from each other and from other varieties of short fiction. John Gardner and Lennis Dunlap offer the following convenient summary in their book *The Forms of Fiction:*

> In general, the Aesopic fable is tough-minded and 'instructive'; it is in this respect quite unlike the typical fairy-tale . . . .

> The form is epigrammatic, extremely economical, and absolutely concrete. It has no room for the elaboration of character or setting and originally had no room for a concluding abstraction to explain meaning . . . .

> The typical parable is realistic in its attitudes and moralistic in its purpose, as is the Aesopic fable; but it need not be cynical or ironic, and its meaning need not be instantly apparent. The characters in a parable are generally human beings, not animals or stones or trees, and certain details in setting and character (both of these are often presented more fully than in the Aesopic fable) may be symbolic.

It is when they no longer insist on a narrowly didactic point that these two forms can enter the territory of the genuine short story. The economy of style and situation that is common in modern narratives gives many of them a parabolic quality, even though they may be much more open-ended than such exemplary old pieces as the New Testament's Prodigal Son and Good Samaritan. Whenever the contours of a story suggest forcibly a summary thematic proposition, we are close to the parable. A modern instance is the compellingly succinct 'Before the Law', included in Kafka's longer work *The Trial* but also published separately. It begins in the plain and pithy way of all parables:

> Before the Law stands a doorkeeper. To this doorkeeper there comes a man from the country who begs for admittance to the Law. But the doorkeeper says he cannot admit the man at present . . .   ·

The rest of the narrative (it is only about a page long) describes the man's vigil as he waits in vain by the entrance year after year. The doorkeeper ignores his pleading. At last, on the point of death, the man asks:

> 'Everyone strives to attain the Law . . . Why is it, then, that all these years no-one but myself has come here to seek admittance?' The doorkeeper sees that the man's end is nigh and that his hearing is failing, so he shouts in his ear: 'No-one but you could gain entry through this door, since it was intended for you alone. And now I am going to shut it.'

Clearly the whole tenor of such a story directs our attention not towards the psychological motivation of an individual character, nor towards any 'real' social circumstances, but towards an implied general statement about the inscrutable nature of authority.

So it is with many other short stories. Is Hawthorne's 'Young Goodman Brown' dominated by the idea that to leave one's faith and community behind means to step into a dark misanthropic vision which can neither be verified nor dismissed? Is Shirley Jackson's 'The Lottery' dominated by the idea that even a placid-seeming community produces violent impulses which it needs to exorcise by ritual sacrifice? To the extent that reductive interpretations are appropriate to the tenor of some stories, those stories are virtually parables. Similarly, there are twentieth-century writers like Malamud ('The Jew-Bird') and Kafka ('Josephine the Singer, or the Mouse-Folk', 'Investigations of a Dog') who invite us to imagine animals with human traits in essentially the same spirit as La Fontaine or Joel Chandler (Uncle Remus) Harris, but without any overt moral lesson attached.

Mixed modes

At their purest, each of these tributary forms represents a distinct and easily recognizable narrative mode. But we find in some stories a confluence of several modes. This is increasingly true in modern fiction, but some antique tales also gain much of their impact by this means.

Take, for instance, Thor's encounter with the magician-giant-king Loki of Utgarð, as related by the medieval Icelandic writer Snorri Sturluson in the Gylfaginning section of his Prose Edda. The whole episode unfolds with a fine sense of the virtues of stylistic understatement and structural compression, and the tone remains consistent. It is compounded, however, of various sorts of narrative, and in this mixture lies the reader's chief pleasure. It is a tale of the gods, with aetiological elements, yet Snorri seems not to be an orthodox mythographer: he is telling us all this, we gather, for our amusement rather than instruction, and Thor is no omnipotent deity but a bewildered muscle-man bested by magic. Utgarð-Loki and his vanishing castle belong more to the world of the *Märchen* than to that of pure myth. There is also in this episode something of the appeal of a tall tale; Thor takes such a mighty draught from his drinking-horn, not knowing its tip has been placed in the sea, that he lowers the tidal level, and so on. The factor which brings these several modes together homogeneously is the consistency of Sturluson's terse manner, epitomized in the repeated formula *Ekki er langt um at gøra,* 'There is no need to make a long story about it'.

Seven centuries later, the fiction of Franz Kafka achieves some of its strange effects by playing off one set of narrative conventions against another. Many of his stories resemble *Märchen,* as Max Lüthi observes:

Their figures, like those of the fairy tale, are not primarily individuals, personalities, characters, but simply figures: doers and receivers of the action. They are no more masters of their destiny than are the figures in the fairy-tale. They move through a world which they do not understand but in which they are nevertheless involved. This they have in common with the figures of the fairy-tale: they do not perceive their relationship to the world about them.

But it is the darker kind of *Märchen* that Kafka conjures up, not the kind in which heroes find everlasting happiness. Although his 'Metamorphosis', for instance, has specific similarities with folklore (traced by Douglas Angus in his article 'Kafka's "Metamorphosis" and "The Beauty and the Beast" Tale'), the author allows no release to his dehumanized character, who remains an outcast. In fact, 'Metamorphosis' is not only a black fairy-story but also a black fable, inverting the usual Aesopic convention. The story begins: 'As Gregor Samsa awoke one morning from uneasy dreams he found himself transformed in his bed into a gigantic insect.' The way in which this bizarre situation is developed, with a matter-of-factness that can turn nightmarish panic into comic pathos, recalls something of the atmosphere of the tall tale, while Gregor's plight gradually takes on as well the dimensions of a psychological parable, illustrating palpably a condition of parasitic dependence within the Samsa family.

'The Ballad of the Sad Cafe' will serve as a final example of the compounding of various narrative types. What really distinguishes this from novels is not its length (*c.* 26,000 words), which, though beyond that of an ordinary short story, is much less than that of an ordinary novel. More important is the fact that its leading characters are not of the sort normally found in extensive narratives but are what the narrator calls 'outlandish people' (a hunchbacked dwarf, a gangling gum-booted cross-eyed woman, and a man flamboyantly vicious in nature - grotesque cartoon shapes, each of them). And moreover, 'The Ballad of the Sad Cafe' is *told* in a way that is totally un-novelistic, being reminiscent rather of several of the modes from which the modern short story derives. The opening pages, taken up chiefly with static description of the town and then of Miss

Amelia, suggest the casually observant manner of a sketch-writer. But another tradition, more important for the story as a whole, is also implicit from the start: the yarn. What Malcolm Cowley says of Sherwood Anderson's best stories, that they 'retain the language, the pace, one might even say the gestures of a man talking unhurriedly to his friends', seems true *a fortiori* of McCullers in 'The Ballad of the Sad Cafe'. From the first few paragraphs we catch the tone of a local story-spinner:

> These August afternoons - when your shift is finished there is absolutely nothing to do; you might as well walk down to the Forks Falls Road and listen to the chain gang.
> However, here in this very town there was once a cafe. . . .

Often this ambling vernacular takes on the comic hyperbole of a tall tale, as in the account of Marvin Macey's villainies ('For years, when he was a boy, he had carried about with him the dried and salted ear of a man he had killed in a razor fight. He had chopped off the tails of squirrels in the pinewoods just to please his fancy . . . '), or the account of the awesome final preparations for the big show-down:

> There were several signs that this was the appointed day, and by ten o'clock the news spread all over the county. Early in the morning Miss Amelia went out and cut down her punching bag. Marvin Macey sat on the back step with a tin can of hog fat between his knees and carefully greased his arms and his legs. A hawk with a bloody breast flew over the town and circled twice around the property of Miss Amelia . . . . Both Miss Amelia and Marvin Macey ate four helpings of half-raw roast for dinner, and then lay down in the afternoon to store up strength.

In addition to the yarn and the sketch, other narrative types are involved too. The strange figure of Cousin Lymon gives the story a fairy-tale dimension: he is like some Rumpelstiltskin in physical appearance, he has an uncanny hypnotic power over the townsfolk, and he makes a magical leap to end the fight. Then there is a ballad element, indicated by the title, by the rhythmic repetition of certain phrases, by the use of a simple idiom to relate the tribulations of unrequited love, and by references to folk music at key points in the narrative: 'the slow song of a Negro' in the background on that evening when Lymon arrives in town, the fragment of song heard in the dark at the time when Amelia learns of Marvin's release from prison ('The tune had no start and no finish and was made up of only three notes which went on and on and on' - suggesting the inextricable involvement of the three main characters with each other), and the chain-gang's chant, mentioned at the beginning and emphasized at the end, a chant 'both somber and joyful' which seems to signify simultaneously the isolation of every person and the ambiguous links between them. Finally 'The Ballad of the Sad Cafe' has a parable-like quality in that it exemplifies some ideas about love set forth in a home-spun homily ('Love is a solitary thing, etc.). All these narrative elements combine in the pervading tone of the story-teller's voice, a tone supple enough to blend pathos and comedy within a tradition to which novelists have seldom sought access.

4
Brevity expanded

The short story shares no clear and common boundary line with the novel. We should examine next some other sorts of prose fiction that intervene between those two polar categories. There are individual narratives of medium length and breadth; there are collections of stories unified by interconnecting themes, motifs, and characters; and there are collections of stories unified within a framing device.

Novella

The word *novella* and its cognates have already been set in a broad perspective near the end of the first chapter, with additional reference to some of its historical inflexions in chapter 2. Difficulties posed by terminology and by different national traditions need not be pursued any further here; detailed accounts are available in sources mentioned previously, or in Harry Steinhauer's article, 'Towards A Definition of the Novella'. But what does deserve consideration at present is, in Henry James's phrase, 'the dimensional ground' of the 'shapely *nouvelle*'. Without reviving the fallacy that fiction is classifiable into absolutely discrete segments, we can agree in identifying some works - increasingly common since the early nineteenth century, and nowadays usually labelled novellas - whose dimensions seem different from those of a normal short story on the one hand and of a normal novel on the other. Arguments for granting independent status to the middling kind of fiction are propounded in two recent monographs in English:

Judith Leibowitz's *Narrative Purpose in the Novella* and Mary Doyle Springer's *Forms of the Modern Novella.*

On the assumption that 'each narrative form has its own developmental methods, its own manner of developing or giving shape to its fictional material', Leibowitz goes on to assert that

> in general terms, this means that the novel's selectivity differs from the short story's because the novel's narrative task is elaboration, whereas the short story's is limitation. And the novella's techniques of selection differ from the other two genres of fiction because its narrative purpose is compression . . . .

She supports her theory by drawing attention to the 'double effect of intensity with expansion', seen as a total aesthetic impression rather than a stylistic device, in such works as James's 'The Bench of Desolation', Hauptmann's 'Bahnwärter Thiel', Mérimée's 'Carmen' and Silone's 'La Volpe e le Camelie', where the compressive quality is achieved by an unwavering thematic focus and an accumulation of structural parallels. It is futile, Leibowitz declares, to suppose that the novella or any other genre can be defined merely by noting the presence of this or that 'characteristic' technique. Such an approach

> fails to consider the purpose for which certain techniques have been used, and therefore does not guide us to an appreciation of their relative importance or to an ability to distinguish differences in their function in different generic contexts.

In the same spirit Springer insists that no distinctive traits can be discovered in the novella 'if we concentrate on parts in isolation (plot, character, diction) without reference to how they "work" in the kind of whole in which they appear and relative to the magnitude of that whole.' Examining several medium-range narratives by Mann, Colette, Lawrence, Crane, Stein and others, she takes the view that a novella's scope is especially fitting for a few kinds of fictional modes whose principle of coherence is most often 'serious or restrainedly tragic, seldom or never . . . comic, though parts are often comical in the service of satire and other forms.' The kind of satire which gravitates towards the novella is that in which 'the object of ridicule is a single one rather than a compendium of the follies of mankind'; 'Cat's Cradle' by Kurt Vonnegut exemplifies this, and even Voltaire's 'Candide', while showing us many sorts of fools and knaves, concentrates on the stupidity of Panglossian optimism. Another mode for which novellas seem suitable is the 'degenerative or pathetic tragedy' (Mann's 'Death in Venice' and James's 'Daisy Miller' being obvious paradigms); 'its relentlessness and the depth of the misery expand it beyond the single episode which often characterizes the short story'. And another is the 'apologue' (by which Springer means a fairly overt and stylized parable - Johnson's 'Rasselas', Conrad's 'Heart of Darkness', Lawrence's 'The Woman Who Rode Away'); in this form, characters *per se* are never our prime concern, since some *idea* shapes the whole. Like Leibowitz, Springer finds that insistent repetition and other elements designed both to intensify and to enlarge the action will very frequently govern the novella form.

In basic accord with these two critics (though he neither uses the term 'novella' nor attempts such a comprehensive theory) is Howard Nemerov, whose essay 'Composition and Fate in the Short Novel' discusses the 'peculiar purity' of structural concentration in works like Dostoevsky's 'Notes from the Underground', Melville's 'Benito Cereno' and Chekhov's 'Ward 6'. Nemerov thinks that this form should be regarded 'not as a compromise between novel and short story, but as something like the ideal and primary form, suggestively allied in simplicity and even in length with the tragedies of antiquity, and dealing in effect with equivalent materials'. Presumably Nemerov does not imply that a novel, being more spacious, is thereby deprived of quasi-tragic potential; *Anna Karenina, Jude the Obscure, Under the Volcano* and other works show the contrary. But certainly it seems to be true that the novella's medial scope enables it to render with especial force the 'degenerative or pathetic' kind of tragedy, as Springer calls it, in which the protagonist's fate is neither heroic nor petty.

We can supplement the remarks of these critics with a point made at the close of the previous chapter, applying it specifically to the novella. For whatever uncertainty may remain concerning the generic status of particular narratives (Melville's 'Bartleby', say, and Joyce's 'The Dead': novellas or short stories?), it does seem to be the case that composite works like Kafka's 'Metamorphosis' and McCullers' 'Ballad of the Sad Cafe' need the balance of strict economy and resonant amplitude which a novella affords. Playing off one mode, one set of narrative conventions, against others is a method requiring usually more than a few pages to implement.

Cycle

Probably the impulse to combine individual tales into larger wholes has its origin in the very nature of imagination itself, a 'coadunating' power as Coleridge described it. Certainly many old story-clusters show that the impulse goes far back into oral tradition, while conventions of the written word have introduced also a practical need to mediate between normal short-story size and normal book size. To group separate stories together cohesively, two sorts of constructive method may be used: internal linking and external framing.

The former method produced in times gone by some composite narratives of courtly and epic quality, such as Malory's *Morte d'Arthur*, with its interconnected Grail romances, or *The Book of Dede Korkut*, a group of heroic legends about the nomadic Oghuz Turks. But in those early cycles there was often a lack of firm structural unity, and the constituent parts were hardly short stories in the modern sense. Our present interest lies rather with the kind discussed by Forrest L. Ingram in his study *Representative Short-Story Cycles of the Twentieth Century* (1971). He defines his subject as 'a book of short stories so linked to each other by their author that the reader's successive experience on various levels of the pattern of the whole significantly modifies his experience of each of its component parts'. Thus characters, settings, leitmotifs, deepen their significance as they recur with variations in one story after another, and moreover a sense of community normally develops through the series. It may be localized in a particular place (Joyce's Dublin, Anderson's Winesburg), or centred on a family (as in Faulkner's *Go Down Moses),* or dispersed through a looser-knit group sharing only an area of social malaise (Moorhouse's *Futility and Other Animals* and its sequel *The Americans, Baby).* 'However this community may be achieved', says Ingram, 'it usually can be said to constitute the central character of a cycle.' While individual protagonists will perhaps appear in several sections of the cycle, and the sections be interrelated chronologically, neither of those connective principles is necessary. Joyce's *Dubliners* deserves to be regarded as a cycle because of its integral patterning and its evocation of Dublin as a 'centre of paralysis', but its stories have no clear temporal relationship with each other nor any characters in common.

Sherwood Anderson's *Winesburg, Ohio* stands as an obvious paradigm of the modern short-story cycle. Its form is clearly between an episodic novel and a mere collection of discrete items. The setting is fairly constant in place and time, and many characters appear in more than one story, with George Willard being present in all but a few. But the tight continuous structure of a novel is deliberately avoided; Anderson said he wanted 'a new looseness' of form to suit the particular quality of his material. His people are lonely, restless, cranky. Social cohesion is absent in their mid-western town. Even momentary communication seldom occurs between any two of them. Winesburg is undergoing a human erosion caused by the winds of change blowing from the cities, by the destabilizing of moral codes, and by the intrinsic thinness of small-town life. The 'new looseness' of *Winesburg, Ohio* can convey with precision and pathos the duality that results: a superficial appearance (and indeed the ideal possibility) of communal wholeness, and an underlying actual separateness. Reinforcing this structural pattern are certain leitmotifs, such as the title image in 'Hands'. Opening the book (except for its prologue), this story concerns the inability of one acutely sensitive and isolated man, Wing Biddlebaum, to express his feelings in words to young George Willard; it includes a painful episode from his past, explaining his emotional agitation; and it ends with a scene in which the central image of his hands becomes imbued with symbolic significance. Always moving nervously and ineffectually, the hands are a perfect focus for Anderson's main theme: they suggest fluttery impulses towards human contact, thwarted both by the individual's timidity and by others' failure to understand and respond. Throughout the ensuing stories, manual gestures continue to be emphasized, whether expressing frustration or despair or aggression.

Sometimes the unifying bonds in a short-story cycle are barely strong enough to distinguish it from an assortment of independent stories. Faulkner's *Go Down Moses* is problematic in this way. It is plainly no novel, and in fact 'the individuality of most of the stories almost demolishes the cohesion of the larger unit', in Ingram's view, yet Faulkner's intention to design the book as a unit is clear. Gradually, as one section follows another with movement back and forth between the present century and the nineteenth, a complex family history emerges obliquely. To grasp the genealogy is to grasp the essential meaning of the whole. But while each story gains greatly from being juxtaposed with the rest, it is also true that one of them, 'The Bear', dominates the volume and is very often read as a separate novella, and that another, 'Pantaloon in Black', does not fit into the family chronicle at all.

Go Down Moses, Winesburg, and numerous other modern short-story cycles such as Eudora Welty's *The Golden Apples* and John Steinbeck's *The Pastures of Heaven* locate their unity of place in some rural region. In this they follow the most notable nineteenth-century prototypes, Turgenev's *A Sportsman's Sketches* and Daudet's *Lettres de Mon Moulin.* But a minority of cycles has a metropolitan context - Frank Moorhouse's work, for example. His prefatory note to his first book states:

> These are interlinked stories and, although the narrative is discontinuous and there is no single plot, the environment and characters are continuous. In some ways, the people in the stories are a tribe; a modern, urban tribe which does not fully recognize itself as a tribe. Some of the people are central members of the tribe while others are hermits who live on the fringe. The shared environment is both internal (anxieties, pleasures and confusions) and external (the houses, streets, hotels and experiences). The central dilemma is that of giving birth, of creating new life.

Given Moorhouse's view of this social area, it would be inappropriate to integrate the episodes into a novel, making their ends meet seamlessly. Discontinuity-in-relationship (between desire and act, lust and tenderness, conception and parturition, libertarian and conformist, younger and older, foreigner and native-born, male and female, Sydney and the bush . . .) is as much a structural and stylistic principle of his writings as it is their theme, and the cycle is accordingly his natural form. A large Australian city in the 1960s may seem a far cry from a midwestern town in the early years of this century, but Moorhouse's fiction and the *Winesburg* stories express fundamentally a similar sense of groping search by isolated characters ('lives flowing past each other', in Anderson's phrase) for an elusive feeling of community.

Framed miscellany

Akin to a cycle is the kind of short-story volume which is rounded off by the use of a framing device. A *Rahmenerzählung* (the German term, now coming into general critical parlance, for a tale within which other tales are set) encloses the components of many old collections, some of them versified (Chaucer's *Canterbury Tales* is an obvious example) but most consisting of prose narratives (the Indian *Panchatantra,* Arabian *Thousand and One Nights,* Italian *Decameron,* Spanish *Conde Lucanor,* Latin *Golden Ass*). Whereas the parts of a cycle are woven into an integral totality, these ancient framed collections comprise a miscellany of narrative types, diverse and discrete. Instead of the sense of community that usually permeates a cycle, linking story to story, a framed miscellany often situates its communal principle in the *Rahmenerzählung:* a group of pilgrims riding together to Canterbury, or a sophisticated company of young raconteurs taking refuge from the Florentine plague. But that did not remain an invariable feature of the miscellany; in Hoffmann's *Die Serapionsbrüder* (1819), instead of being societal, the framing principle is subjectively individual: each narrator relates something seen with his *inner* eye. And besides, it is not in the group of narrators as such that any miscellany's real unity lies. The framing device is often more or less perfunctory, a conventional pretext for assembling different items. Holding such collections together in a more pervasive way is their author's fascination with the manifold roots and branches of narration itself.

A modern miscellany will serve to illustrate this: Christina Stead's undeservedly neglected book *The Salzburg Tales* (1934). Its animating interest in all aspects of tale-telling appears first in the authorial prologue, 'The Personages', where Stead distinguishes between particular kinds of stories favoured by different people and between the individual qualities of their imaginations or manners of speaking. There is the

Frenchwoman, with her 'firm caressing voice':

> to everything she said she gave an aphoristic turn; her conversation disarmed the jealous, dismayed the dull and sharpened with salt the wit of the witty . . . In company she had no equal; she was benevolent and polished in repartee, in anecdote pithy and wise, and in her tales circumstantial and rotund with a long line of development and a sentimental conclusion.

By way of contrast the Doctress 'preferred scandalous stories and her ideas came out of a slipshod imagination, with an evident intention of pleasing only herself . . . ' So the characterizations continue, often suggesting directly how and why these folk like to talk or listen. The Lawyer is impelled by a greed for gossip; the Foreign Correspondent speaks 'with compressed visionary epithets, as if his imagination flowered impetuously, quicker than the tongue'; the Centenarist 'was full of tales as the poets of Persia: he unwound endlessly his fabrics, as from a spool the silks of Arabia'; the Danish Woman 'talked all day and recounted hundreds of tales, mostly improbable, like a female Munchhausen'; the Old Man 'liked company and joined in all the conversations to show he was a spark and an accomplished trifler'; the Public Stenographer enlivens and enlarges her small dull existence with 'anecdotes of the comic, pathetic and marvellous'; the Translator, who is 'bitter, stinging with a thousand imagined affronts, and, cruel, ready for a thousand expected attacks', would 'run down even his dearest friends for the pleasure of saying something original on his own account'; the Police Commissioner cultivates literary skills as one of several means to an end: 'He had improved his manne's, taken an eyeglass, studied fine eating, invented a few dishes, written two romances and a book of aphorisms and learned to seem wise by ignoring questions'; the Broker's tongue 'wallowed through a heavy swell of epithets', and so on, often in more detail.

It is not only in these scattered introductory comments in the frame but also through further details in the ensuing collection that Stead expresses her curiosity about sources and forms of fiction. The tales appear now as products of place, now as products of personality. In one of them a scandal-monger observes that malicious tattle, so rife in his village, seems to pertain to the very locality - topical talk in the most basic sense. 'Those histories', he says, 'spring up here spontaneously; it is like the feverish, foul air of decay, or a loathsome deposit left by the old mountain lake that infects the air, a melancholy or ague which every one of us gets eventually.' In another story, another village teems with superstitions and credulous fancies that nourish any rumour; in another, provincial Périgord is said to have as its mistress 'bell-tongued Calliope', who 'tells many a ribald pasquinade or minor pomp, and pieces together with florid interludes village tales whose tissues long ago fell in tatters in the sun.' There is a more personal derivation for some of the other stories, such as the one recounted by the Musical Critic, who confesses to being 'an inveterate and shameless eavesdropper': 'I listen at the doors of rooms, I pussyfoot along the corridors, I read private letters . . . I chortle over the butt-end of a conversation, and pick up chance remarks uttered as I pass in the street.'

And so it goes on, with narrator after narrator and character after character revealing motivation after motivation. But the author's preoccupation with fictional processes is most comprehensively evinced in the great variety of the tales themselves - simple and sophisticated, laconic and grandiloquent, refined and raw . . . a full range is there, embracing virtually every mode or sub-genre of the short story.

The framed miscellany is not always so distinct from the short-story cycle. Alphonse Daudet's *Lettres de Mon Moulin* (1869) seems casually conjoined, and comprises a heterogeneous assortment of narrative types - sketches, yarns, fables, 'ballades en prose' - set into an informal frame. Yet its tone is more uniform, its narrative scope more constricted, than in a true miscellany. Despite the structural looseness, its affinity lies rather with the cycle form; Daudet evokes piecemeal the life of a regional community in Provence with much the same kind of cumulative effect as Anderson conveys in *Winesburg, Ohio*.

5
Essential qualities?

Essays on the short story began to appear frequently during the first two decades of this century, especially in America. These repeat unanimously the view that it is a distinctive genre whose uniqueness lies in three related qualities: it makes a single impression on the reader, it does so by concentrating on a crisis, and it makes that crisis pivotal in a controlled plot. Although this attractively neat triad did not become common doctrine until about 1900, it derived from remarks made much earlier by the pioneer theorist Edgar Allan Poe.

'Unity of impression'
Reviewing some of Nathaniel Hawthorne's fiction in 1842, Poe asserted that the chief formal property of 'the short prose tale' was 'unity of impression', which he regarded as a product of conscious artistry; the author first 'conceived, with deliberate care, a certain unique or single effect to be wrought out', and then devised an appropriate narrative vehicle for conveying that. Taken up by Brander Matthews ('The Philosophy of the Short-story', 1884) and others, this emphasis on singleness of effect and economy of means has until recently gained wide acceptance. And of course it is true, if not truistic, to say that lapses and laxities will probably be damaging in a brief narrative, being relatively more prominent there than in a longer one. V.S. Pritchett glosses what is incontestable in Poe's dictum when he remarks: 'The wrong word, a misplaced paragraph, an inadequate phrase or a convenient explanation, start

fatal leaks in this kind of writing, which is formally very close to poetry. It must be totally sustained.' But Poe's conception of unity, claiming to go further than that, becomes too limited to cover all short stories. For one thing, his implication that formal unity should always be a matter of 'deliberate care' is very dubious. From a reading of Kafka's diaries and letters, which incorporate many embryonic stories and a few fully realized ones, it is clear that some of his fictions were no more deliberately wrought than dreams, than Coleridge's 'Kubla Khan' or Browning's 'Childe Roland'. While Kafka's work may represent an extreme, the experience of writers generally still does not seem to indicate that composing an impressive story need involve any mechanical contrivance. And the experience of readers generally belies the notion that any strict tonal consistency or monochromatic emotional range is requisite for a story to be an aesthetically satisfying whole. What makes many of Chekhov's narratives, for instance, so moving in an unsentimentally poignant way is surely that they establish a tensile balance between comedy and pathos. Gogol's seminal story 'The Overcoat' is similarly mixed: as one of its translators, Ronald Wilks, remarks, 'now it is chatty and friendly, now ironical, now completely impersonal, now sentimental. And this strange medley is shot with witty anecdotes and startling asides which transfer the whole action to another plane of reality.' There are indeed many fine stories whose appeal seems to stem mainly from their very lack of a 'single effect', as shown earlier in discussing 'The Ballad of the Sad Cafe', where the total unified impact is achieved by an interplay of several modes. And if 'unity of impression' is to be interpreted flexibly enough to include that kind of multiplex narrative, it can hardly be denied to novels too: unity is not so simply correlated with brevity as Poe suggests.

'*Moment of crisis*'
A Dictionary of Literary Terms, edited by Sylvan Barnet *et al.*

(London, 1964), notes that 'most frequently a short-story writer of the nineteenth or twentieth centuries focuses on a single
character in a single episode, and rather than tracing his development, reveals him at a particular moment'; and as Theodore
Stroud observes in his essay 'A Critical Approach to the Short
Story', this moment is frequently one at which the character
undergoes some decisive change in attitude or understanding,
as when Olga, in Chekhov's 'The Grasshopper', suddenly recog-
nized her husband's true worth and her acute need of him just
as he dies.

James Joyce was keenly aware of the importance of these
critical revelations in some of his own stories. He even applied
to them a special technical term, 'epiphany' (a showing-forth).
At the end of the final story in *The Dubliners*, 'The Dead',
Gabriel is assailed for the first time with 'a shameful consciousness of his own person ... He saw himself as a ludicrous
figure.' Another story, 'Araby', leads similarly to a painful
flash of self-awareness for the narrator. He begins by describing the 'blind' street where he lived as a boy (the significant
adjective appears twice in the first two sentences), and where
the houses 'gazed at one another with brown imperturbable
faces'. After depicting his adolescent romanticizing and abrupt
disillusionment, he concludes: 'Gazing up into the darkness I
saw myself as a creature driven and derided by vanity; and my
eyes burned with anguish and anger.'

But common though this pattern is in short stories, the personal crisis-point is not at all necessary. If a significant revelation does occur, it *may* involve a perceived moment of truth for
a character, but frequently it will be for readers only. Joyce's
'Clay' is an example of the latter. It simply describes a simple
woman's enjoyment of Hallow-e'en: a special tea with the
women she works with at a laundry, and a visit to her brother
and his family. To Maria it is all 'pleasant'; she 'laughed and
laughed', she 'said they were all very good to her', etc. But we
see more than she does. We see the pathetic constriction and

isolation of her existence, and others' lack of sensitivity towards her. Maria doesn't understand the practical joke that is played on her by the next-door girls while she is blindfolded; it's the reader who identifies the 'soft wet substance' she touches with the story's title image, and who recognizes that this represents Maria's portion in life. She herself remains uncomprehending.

There are examples of both sorts in Katherine Mansfield's work: stories such as 'Bliss' and 'Miss Brill' show people at a crucial point of new self-knowledge, but in 'Psychology' the reader comes to see that the main characters, for all their imagined candour, cannot perceive the true nature of their relationship - that in fact they will continue to deceive themselves, Prufrock-like in lacking 'the strength to force the moment to its crisis'. Hemingway, too, writes stories of both sorts. Often the focus is on a situation where someone is critically tested; in 'The Short Happy Life of Francis Macomber' Macomber has failed one trial before the narrative begins, but redeems himself when another occurs, triumphing not only over his own fear but over those who have treated him contemptuously because of his earlier failure. Similarly some Hemingway stories show a person being initiated into adulthood, or a person, who having chosen, is alone with the consequences of what he has done or failed to do; the two appear together in 'The Killers', which presents Andreson's stoical confrontation of his imminent death and also the moment when young Nick becomes aware of certain implacable facts of life - cruelty, indifference to suffering, the essential isolation of human beings. But there is no moment of crisis in some of Hemingway's most memorable fiction. Virtually nothing happens in 'A Clean, Well-lighted Place', and indeed that nothing, *nada,* is precisely what the story is about. And there are numerous stories by other writers, for instance Fielding Dawson's account of inconclusive pub encounters, which do not raise the action, external or internal, to any momentous peak.

Moreover, what makes some stories linger in the mind is that we are left uncertain about the nature and extent of the revelation, peak of awareness, that a character has apparently experienced. We sense that, while there has indeed been an important shift of perspective in her/his view of things, its significance may not yet have been fully apprehended by that character. This is true of some fine stories by Nadine Gordimer; in a thoughtful essay on her work, Kevin Magarey remarks that what the reader finally understands is often also 'in the consciousness of actors or narrator, but subliminally'. Sometimes, indeed, even a most attentive reader could hardly indicate very precisely what the climatic insight amounts to, palpable though its importance may be. 'Friday's Footprint', the title piece in one of Gordimer's books, culminates in a moment when Rita arrives at the brink of recognizing *something* about herself, about her present marriage, about her previous marriage, about the essence of her relationship with both husbands. But the denouement is not quite completed; at the end she is still struggling with the knot of her feelings, and so is the reader.

Some narratives that do seem at first to hinge on a personal crisis-point are in fact adumbrating the pattern only to subvert it. Henry James's 'The Beast in the Jungle' illustrates this latter type in a way that approaches parody of the moment-of-crisis story: it is deliberately anti-climactic, building up to the stage when something does *not* change substantially in the main character's mind. John Marcher himself fails to recognize the crisis for what it is. He has spent his life waiting for some thrilling revelation, for the Beast to appear; but the Beast springs unseen when Marcher overlooks his final opportunity to extricate himself from the petty self-absorption which has enclosed his whole being. The habit of egotism is so entrenched that he still cannot see his long-suffering friend May as more than a convenient adjunct to himself. The final few pages do, it is true, record a kind of belated anagnorisis when 'everything fell together': Marcher becomes painfully conscious of his loss as he stands beside May's grave. Yet even then he apparently remains less than fully aware of his own nature and situation, and we can hardly suppose that thenceforth his life's direction will be altered.

'Symmetry of design'

In his influential 1884 essay, elaborating on Poe's principles, Brander Matthews declared that 'symmetry of design' was a *sine qua non* in the short story. Insistence on this quality accords with his view that a short story is almost null if it has no plot. And as recently as 1945 A.L. Bader firmly endorsed that view: plot is always basic, he argued, in the modern short story, and the narrative structure is always derived from conflict, sequential action, and resolution. Similarly Somerset Maugham and others have said that Aristotle's dictum about the need for a beginning, a middle and an end applies as axiomatically to the short story as to the drama or novel, and we have already noted, in the first chapter, that there appears to be a basic aesthetic principle underlying that desideratum. But while symmetrical design of some sort will frequently be present in a short story, it is patently not a property that belongs to that form in any distinctive indispensable way. Insistence on symmetry began with Poe, and has more to do with his own psychic obsessions than with any essential qualities of the genre. Plot-hatching is part of his preoccupation with detective puzzles, and with situations and imagery of enclosure - chambers, pits, walled cavities, vaults.

There are indeed two good reasons for discarding 'symmetry of design' as a definitive term in critical parlance about the short story. One is that regarding symmetry as requisite has not helped critics to talk discriminatingly about the structure of stories in which it actually is present; the other is that it has impeded recognition of the fact that in many good stories symmetry is not present at all.

To enlarge on the first point: an excessive emphasis on ingenious plotting (Matthews listed 'ingenuity' among the 'chief requisites' of the short story), and especially a relish for the Final Twist as exemplified most notoriously in the writings of O. Henry, is particularly unfortunate since it has tended to provoke a reactive critical disparagement of all surprise endings, some of which are however not manipulative devices but ways of elucidating meanings latent in the whole narrative. Guy de Maupassant's 'La Parure' ('The Necklace') exemplifies this. Its main character, Mme Loisel, is the wife of a small-time civil servant; she yearns for a life of luxury, especially for expensive clothes and jewellery, and is acutely irritable because of her husband's meagre income. These feelings come to a head when the couple is invited to an official reception. She makes such a fuss over having nothing to adorn herself with that they borrow a diamond necklace from a more affluent acquaintance. The necklace is lost; after frenetic efforts they manage to borrow a huge sum, buy a replacement and return that (without revealing the mishap) to the lender of the necklace. M. and Mme Loisel spend the next decade in exhausting work to pay off the enormous debt. Only after that long period of expiation does the woman happen to learn that the borrowed necklace was merely a cheap imitation. This sudden revelation at its close has brought the story into disfavour with some critics. Roger Colet, for instance, omits 'La Parure' from his recent selection of Maupassant's fiction, implying in a dismissive reference to it that its plot is factitious. But there is more to it than that, as Cleanth Brooks and Robert Penn Warren show in their annotated anthology *Understanding Fiction,* which includes and discusses 'La Parure' in the same section as O. Henry's well known story 'The Furnished Room'. This latter concerns a young man's failure to find his lost sweetheart. For months he has searched for her in the big city, and as the narration opens he is wearily taking a room in one of the many old houses of New York's lower West Side. To the landlady he puts the question that he has asked a thousand times elsewhere: has she had among her transient lodgers a certain young actress, fair, of medium height, etc., with a mole by her left eyebrow? No, the landlady 'can't call that one to mind'. Dispirited, he sinks into a dull reverie - which is suddenly invaded by a scent of mignonette: his sweetheart's perfume! Rushing downstairs, he asks the landlady who had rented the room previously. But none of the tenants she describes as having occupied it recently could have been the woman he seeks. When he returns to the room, the scent has gone. Then, after blocking every crevice, he turns on the gas. Meanwhile the landlady is telling a friend of hers that the troublesome third-floor room has been rented out to a young man. No, she had not told him about the suicide there a week before. That dead girl had been 'a pretty slip of a colleen to be killin' herself wid the gas'; handsome, indeed, 'but for that mole she had a-growin' by her left eyebrow'.

As Brooks and Warren remark, O. Henry seems here to be guilty of artistic dishonesty. Characterization, and therefore motivation, remain sketchy, and the story amounts merely to a contrived demonstration of 'the irony of fate'. The withheld information, the lie, is for the reader's benefit only; presumably if the landlady had told the young man the truth, that the girl was dead etc., his reaction would have been just as despairing. The ending provides at most an illusion of significance. But in Maupassant's story the surprising turn at the end reveals more than just a hidden fact, a sad irony; it brings to the surface the real significance of the foregoing action. The lost jewels were, after all, only paste, worthless baubles. But so, in a sense, is the 'real' necklace which cost Mme Loisel so much (not only in money) to pay off. The story's theme has to do with true and false values, and the falsity of the lost article becomes symbolic of the basic situation. In retrospect the loss of the jewels appears not so much a terrible misfortune as a disguised blessing.

Criticism needs to distinguish, then, between the merely

tricky ending and the ending which jolts us into perceiving something fundamental about what we have been reading. It is of no relevance to look for symmetrical plot-design, which in itself cannot be correlated with degrees of artistry.

In fairness to O. Henry, one should add that his use of final surprises sometimes has a more respectable function than in his falsely sentimental piece 'The Furnished Room'. Boris Eichenbaum, the Russian formalist critic, credits O. Henry with bringing the nineteenth-century American short story to the phase of structural parody, thus opening the way for a regeneration of the genre. As cultivated by O. Henry's predecessors, says Eichenbaum, the short story tends to amass its weight like an anecdote towards the conclusion, 'towards the maximal unexpectedness of a finale concentrating around itself all that has preceded it'. O. Henry lays bare this structural pattern by playful emphasis on the devices associated with it; he 'annotates the progress of the plot, taking each instance as an opportunity for introducing literary irony, for destroying the illusion of authenticity, for parodying a cliché, for making palpable the conventionality of art, or showing how the story is put together. The author time and again intrudes into the events of his own story and engages the reader in literary conversation, turning the story into a feuilleton'. Written half a century ago, Eichenbaum's long and important essay is now available in an English translation as 'O. Henry and the Theory of the Short Story' in *Readings in Russian Poetics,* (ed. Matejka and Pomorska.)

The second reason for resisting Aristotelian requirements in short-story criticism is that the action of a short story, though hardly of a more extended composition, need have no completed pattern at all. It may be virtually without start or finish, representing only a state of affairs rather than a sequence of events. This is generally true of the work of some writers; Galsworthy said Chekhov's stories are 'all middle, like a tortoise', and Chekhov himself once remarked: 'I think that when one has finished writing a short story one should delete the beginning and the end'. In discarding patterns of enclosure the short-story writer can perhaps discover a freedom and imaginative truth inherent in this genre. Elizabeth Bowen declares that 'the short story, free from the *longeurs* of the novel, is also exempt from the novel's conclusiveness - too often forced and false'. And although a few writers have continued to opt for neatly pointed plots ('I preferred', says Somerset Maugham, 'to end my stories with a full-stop rather than with a straggle of dots'), there has been a growing tendency during the present century for short stories to be 'all middle', to avoid structural complications in general and terminal climaxes in particular.

With simple directness Robert Creeley expressed this freer sense of form in prefacing his 1953 book of short fiction, *The Gold Diggers*:

> Whereas the novel is a continuum, of necessity, chapter to chapter, the story can escape some of that obligation, and function exactly in terms of whatever emotion best can serve it.
>
> The story has no time finally. Or it hasn't here. Its shape, if form can be so thought of, is a sphere, an egg of obdurate kind. The only possible reason for its existence is that it has, in itself, the fact of reality and the pressure. There, in short, is its form - no matter how random and broken that will seem. The old assumptions of beginning and end - those very neat assertions - have fallen away completely in a place where the only actuality is life, the only end (never realized) death, and the only value, what love one can manage.
>
> It is impossible to think otherwise, or at least I have found it so. I begin where I can, and end when I see the whole thing returning.

In a stricter sense there is a type of story, more and more common in modern fiction, which could not exist if it had a developing plot in the old manner. Samuel F. Pickering mentions a few examples in a review of some recent American short-story anthologies:

> In Patricia Griffith's 'Nights at O'Rear's' (O'Rear's is a drive-in restaurant in a small Texas town), the idle young in their cars, forever circling the drive-in, can be taken as a metaphor for the story's form. In its end is its beginning and in its beginning is its end; the divisions of the story are inseparable and there is no progression between them. Wright Morris's 'Magic' confuses the reader by describing a psychological world in which past, present and future are only separated from one another. Other stories such as Tillie Olson's 'Raqua I' and Jonathan Strong's 'Patients' examine the non-sequential world of the mentally ill.

Pickering does not much like stores of this kind; they 'luxuriate in stasis', he says. But unless we turn our back on work by some of the most eminent living fiction-writers, there can be no gainsaying the fact that stasis has become very common in modern stories. 'Stasis' is perhaps a misnomer in most cases, since some activity takes place. Rather than being inert, the character shows himself unable or unwilling to alter his situation; the movement is of a treadmill sort or suggests continuous transit without a foreseeable re-entry into social relationships. This inconclusiveness becomes a meaningful principle of structure. Only the most rigid dogmatism would lead one to regard as faultily fragmentary a piece like Ted Hughes's 'Snow', narrated by someone whose situation is totally mysterious to himself and us because he is literally surrounded by blankness; perhaps he is in a post-mortem limbo, or . . .? Similarly inconclusive situations pervade Jorge Luis Borges's 'The Gods' Script', in which the sole character merely meditates (interminably, we are led to suppose) on the idea of endlessness, and John Barth's 'The Night-Sea Journey', a monologue by a swimming creature - Human? Piscine? Spermatic? - who is in some sort of oceanic expanse but unaware of his goal or meaning, if any.

This kind of narrative, open at both ends, frequently centres on a certain character-type: the bird-of-passage figure whose significance depends on the fact that his origins and destinations are beyond the narrative's scope. The first (titular) story of McCullers' collection *The Ballad of the Sad Cafe* gets under way with the arrival of Lymon the stranger; when asked, 'Where you come from?' he replies simply, 'I was travelling'. And at the end of the last story in the same volume a bystander makes this comment on the enigmatic main character, who has just made his exit: 'He sure has done a lot of travelling.' The nomadic pattern suggested there (and metaphorically echoed by that tune in 'The Ballad' which 'had no start and no finish') is found time and again in the work of many different writers, and conveys something that the short story can perhaps achieve more finely than any other literary form. By being virtually plotless, narratives of the kind that we have just been considering can make salient a quality which William James came to recognize even in the elaborate tales written by his brother; these gave, he said,

> an impression like that we often get of people in life: their orbits come out of space and lay themselves for a short time along ours, and then off they whirl again into the unknown, leaving us with little more than an impression of their reality and a feeling of baffled curiosity as to the mystery of the beginning and end of their being.

Bibliography

General books of short-story criticism

Bates, H.E., *The Modern Short Story,* London, 1941.
  Selective historical account of the genre, beginning with
  Poe and Gogol; very readable.
Beachcroft, T.O., *The Modest Art: A Survey of the Short
  Story in English,* London, 1968.
  Concentrates in fact on the short story in England, and is
  not much concerned with theoretical issues.
Bungert, Hans (ed.), *Die Amerikanische Short Story: Theorie
  und Entwicklung,* Darmstadt, 1972.
  An anthology of useful material, most of it in English.
Gardner, John, and Dunlap, Lennis (eds), *The Forms of Fic-
  tion,* New York, 1962.
  One of many American short-story collections intended for
  students; this one has a more thorough introductory essay
  than most.
Kilchenmann, Ruth J., *Die Kurzgeschichte: Formen und
  Entwicklung,* Stuttgart, 1967.
  An interesting demonstration of the difficulty of distinguish-
  ing categorically between the short story and the German
  Novelle.
Kumar, Shiv K., and McKean, Keith (eds), *Critical Ap-
  proaches to Fiction,* New York, 1968.
  Includes reprinted articles on the short story by Bader,
  Stroud, West, Marcus and Welty.

Matthews, Brander, *The Philosophy of The Short Story*, New York, 1901.

Strongly influenced by Poe, this booklet was the first critical study of the form in English. In a briefer version, it first appeared in *The Saturday Review* (London) in 1884. Reprinted by Bungert and (in extract) by Summers.

O'Connor, Frank, *The Lonely Voice: A Study of the Short Story*, New York, 1963.

One of the very few studies offering general remarks about the form itself in addition to commentaries on the work of several short-story writers.

O'Faolain, Sean, *The Short Story*, New York, 1951.

Lucid, illuminating, informal discussion of the craft of short fiction.

Summers, Hollis (ed.), *Discussions of the Short Story*, Boston, 1963.

Includes helpful brief essays by Poe, Matthews, Bader and others.

Trask, Georgianne, and Burkhart, Charles (eds), *Storytellers and Their Art*, New York, 1963.

Anthology which brings together 'what writers of the short story have said about it'.

Ancillary and specialized studies

(a) Books

Bennett, E.K., and Waidson, H.M., *A History of the German Novelle*, Cambridge, 1961 (2nd edn).

Castex, Pierre-Georges, *Le Conte Fantastique en France de Nodier à Maupassant*, Paris, 1951.

George, Albert J., *Short Fiction in France: 1800-1850*, Syracuse, 1964.

Gerhardt, Mia I., *The Art of Story-Telling: A Literary Study of the Thousand and One Nights*, Leiden, 1963.

Ingram, Forrest L., *Representative Short-Story Cycles of the Twentieth Century*, The Hague, 1971.

Jolles, André, *Einfache Formen,* Halle, 1956 (2nd edn). Translated into French by Antoine Marie Buguet as *Formes Simples,* Paris, 1972.

Leibowitz, Judith, *Narrative Purpose in the Novella,* The Hague, 1974.

Lüthi, Max, *Once Upon a Time: On the Nature of Fairy Tales,* New York, 1970.

Pattee, F.W., *The Development of the American Short Story: An Historical Survey,* New York, 1923 (reprinted 1966).

Prince, Gerald, *A Grammar of Stories,* The Hague, 1973.

Propp, Vladimir J., *Morphology of the Folk Tale,* Bloomington, 1958 (a translation of the 1928 Russian original). Translated into French as *Morphologie du Conte,* Paris, 1970.

Springer, Mary Doyle, *Forms of the Modern Novella,* Chicago, 1975.

Thalmann, Marianne, *The Romantic Fairy Tale: Seeds of Surrealism* (translated by Mary B. Corcoran), Ann Arbor, 1964.

Trenkner, Sophie, *The Greek Novella in the Classical Period,* Cambridge, 1958.

(b) *Articles and parts of books*

Angus, Douglas, 'Kafka's "Metamorphosis" and "The Beauty and the Beast" Tale', *Journal of English and Germanic Philology,* liii (1954), pp. 69-71.

Bader, A.L., 'The Structure of the Modern Short Story', *College English,* vii (1945), pp. 86-92; reprinted in the collections by Summers and by Kumar and McKean.

Bergonzi, Bernard, 'Appendix on the Short Story', in *The Situation of the Novel,* London, 1970.

Eichenbaum, Boris, 'O. Henry and the Theory of the Short Story', in *Readings in Russian Poetics: Formalist and Structuralist Views,* edited by Ladislav Matejka and Krystyna Pomorska, Cambridge, Mass., 1971, pp. 227-70.

Engstrom, Alfred G., 'The Formal Short Story in France and Its Development Before 1850', *Studies in Philology,* xlii (1945), pp. 627-39.

Friedman, Norman, 'What Makes a Short Story Short?', *Modern Fiction Studies,* iv (1958), pp. 103-17.

Gillespie, Gerald, 'Novella, Nouvelle, Novelle, Short Novel? - A Review of Terms', *Neophilologus,* li (1967), pp. 117-27 and 225-30.

Magarey, Kevin, 'Cutting the Jewel: Facets of Art in Nadine Gordimer's Short Stories', *Southern Review,* vii (1974), pp. 3-28.

Marler, Robert F., 'From Tale to Short Story: The Emergence of a New Genre in the 1850s', *American Literature,* xlvi (1974), pp. 153-69.

Mercier, Vivian, 'The Irish Short Story and Oral Tradition', in *The Celtic Cross: Studies in Irish Culture and Literature,* edited by Ray B. Browne *et al.,* Lafayette, Ind., 1964, pp. 98-116.

Nemerov, Howard, 'Composition and Fate in the Short Novel', in *Poetry and Fiction,* New Brunswick, N.J., 1963, pp. 229-45.

Schlauch, Margaret, 'English Short Fiction in the Fifteenth and Sixteenth Centuries', *Studies in Short Fiction,* iii (1966), pp. 393-434.

Shklovsky, Victor, 'La Construction de la Nouvelle et du Roman', in *Théorie de la Littérature,* edited by Tzvetan Todorov, Paris, 1965, pp. 170-96.

Steinhauer, Harry, 'Towards a Definition of the Novella', *Seminar,* vi (1970), pp. 154-74.

Stroud, Theodore A., 'A Critical Approach to the Short Story', *Journal of General Education,* ix (1956), pp. 91-100; reprinted in the collection by Kumar and McKean.

Todorov, Tzvetan, 'The Structuralist Analysis of Literature: The Tales of Henry James', in *Structuralism: An Introduction,* edited by David Robey, Oxford, 1973, pp. 73-103.

Tolkien, J.R.R., 'On Fairy-Stories', in *Tree and Leaf,* London, 1964, pp. 11-70.

Tynjanov, Jurij, 'On Literary Evolution', in *Readings in Russian Poetics: Formalist and Structuralist View,* edited by Ladislav Matejka and Krystyna Pomorska, Cambridge, Mass., 1971, pp. 66-78.

Index

Addison, Joseph, 22, 31
Aesop, 16
Anderson, Sherwood, 40, 47-8, 49, 53
Angus, Douglas, 68
Apuleius, 16, 50
Aristides of Miletus, 16
Aristotle, 6, 10, 59
Arnim, Achim von, 23
Auerbach, Erich, 19

Babrius, 16
Bader, A.L., 59, 67, 68
Balzac, Honoré de, 24
Barnet, Sylvan, 55
Barth, John, 64
Bates, H.E., 2, 24, 26, 66
Battle of Maldon, The, 19
Beachcroft, T.O., 66
Benedict, Ruth, 35
Benet, Stephen Vincent, 33
Bennett, E.K., 23, 67
Bergonzi, Bernard, 1, 68
Boas, Franz, 35
Baccaccio, Giovanni, 11, 12, 19-22, 50

Book of Dede Korkut, The, 46
Book of Sindibad, The, 18
Book of the Wiles of Women, The, 18
Borges, Jorge Luis, 7, 64
Bowen, Elizabeth, 62
Bremond, Claude, 3, 5, 36
Brentano, Clemens, 23
Brooks, Cleanth, 60, 61
Browning, Robert, 55
Buber, Martin, 8
Bungert, Hans, 66
Burkhart, Charles, 67
Byron, George Gordon, Lord, 27

Castex, P.-G., 35, 67
Cervantes, Miguel de, 11, 22
Chaucer, Geoffrey, 19, 50
Chekhov, Anton, 45, 55, 56, 62-3
Chesterfield, Philip Stanhope, Earl of, 11

Coleridge, Samuel Taylor, 27, 46, 55
Colette, Sidonie-Gabrielle, 44
Conde Lucanor, El, 50
Conrad, Joseph, 11, 45
Coover, Robert, 7
Cowley, Malcolm, 40
Crane, Stephen, 44
Creeley, Robert, 63

Danto, Arthur C., 6
Daudet, Alphonse, 24, 49, 52
Dawson, Fielding, 9, 57
Diderot, Denis, 22
Dostoevsky, Fyodor, 45
Dunlap, Lennis, 36, 66

Edgerton, Franklin, 18
Eichenbaum, Boris, 3, 62, 68
Engstrom, Alfred G., 8, 68
Faulkner, William, 47, 48
Fenton, Geoffrey, 22
Flaubert, Gustave, 8, 24
Forster, E.M., 4
France, Marie de, 19
Friedman, Norman, 69
Fry, Christopher, 17

Galsworthy, John, 62
Gardner, John, 36, 66
Gautier, Théophile, 24
George, Albert J., 12, 67

Gerhardt, Mia I., 67
Gillespie, Gerald, 10, 69
Gogol, Nikolai, 24, 55, 66
Gold, Herbert, 5
Gordimer, Nadine, 58
Greimas, A.J., 36
Griffith, Patricia, 64
Grimm, Brothers, 23, 34

Hall, Joseph, 31
Harris, Joel Chandler, 38
Harte, Bret, 26
Hauptmann, Gerhart, 44
Hawthorne, Nathaniel, 9, 25, 29, 38, 54
Hemingway, Ernest, 9, 57
Henry, O., 60-2
Heyse, Paul, 12
Hoffmann, E.T.A., 23, 34-5, 50
Hrafnkels saga, 19
Hughes, Ted, 64

Ingram, Forrest L., 47-8, 67
Irving, Washington, 25, 30-1

Jackson, Shirley, 38
James, Henry, 9, 43, 44, 45, 58-9, 65
James, William, 65
Johnson, Samuel, 45
Jolles, Andre, 32, 67

Joyce, James, 28, 32, 46, 47, 56-7

Kafka, Franz, 7, 37-8, 39-40, 46, 55
Keats, John, 28
Keller, Grottfried, 23
Kilchenmann, Ruth J., 13, 66
Klein, Johannes, 13, 22
Kleist, Heinrich von, 11, 23
Kumar, Shiv K., 66

La Bruyère, Jean de, 22, 31
La Fontaine, Jean de, 12, 17, 38
Lamb, Charles, 31
Lawrence, D.H., 12, 44, 45
Lawson, Henry, 32
Leibowitz, Judith, 44, 68
Lévi-Strauss, Claude, 35
Luthi, Max, 39, 68

McCullers, Carson, 40-2, 46, 65
McKean, Keith, 66
Magarey, Kevin, 58, 69
Malamud, Bernard, 38
Malory, Sir Thomas, 46
Mann, Thomas, 32, 44, 45
Mansfield, Katherine, 32, 57
Marcus, Mordecai, 66
Marler, Robert F., 25, 69

Matthews, Brander, 4, 54, 59, 60, 67
Maugham, W. Somerset, 9, 59, 63
Maupassant, Guy de, 12, 17, 24, 60-1
Melville, Herman, 25, 26, 45, 46
Mercier, Vivian, 35, 69
Mérimée, Prosper, 11, 12, 24, 44
Morkinskinna, 19
Moore, George, 35
Moorhouse, Frank, 47, 49
Morris, Wright, 64
Musset, Alfred de, 12

Navarre, Marguerite de, 11, 21
Nemerov, Howard, 2, 45, 69
Nerval, Gérard de, 27, 35
Nodier, Charles, 12, 35
North, Thomas, 18

O'Connor, Frank, 2, 27, 67
O'Faolain, Sean, 2, 67
Olson, Tillie, 64
Orwell, George, 31
Overbury, Thomas, 31

Painter, William, 22
Panchatantra, 18, 50
Pater, Walter, 31
Pattee, Fred Lewis, 25, 68

Perrault, Charles, 34
Petronius, 16-17
Pettie, George, 11, 22
Phaedrus, 16
Pickering, Samuel F., 63
Plath, Sylvia, 7
Poe, Edgar Allan, 1, 9, 25, 28, 29, 54-5, 59, 66, 67
Prince, Gerald, 5, 6, 68
Pritchett, V.S., 54
Propp, Vladimir, 3, 35-6, 68
Pushkin, Alexander, 24

Rourke, Constance, 27

Salisbury, John of, 17
Sargeson, Frank, 10
Saroyan, William, 9
Schlauch, Margaret, 69
Shklovsky, Victor, 3, 69
Silone, Ignazio, 44
Sir Launfal, 19
Springer, Mary Doyle, 44-5, 68
Stead, Christina, 50-2
Steele, Richard, 22, 31
Stein, Gertrude, 44
Steinbeck, John, 49
Steinhauer, Harry, 43, 69
Stifter, Adalbert, 23
Storm, Theodor, 23
Strong, Jonathan, 64
Stroud, Theodore, 56, 66, 69

Sturluson, Snorri, 19, 39
Summers, Hollis, 67

Thalmann, Marianne, 23, 68
Theophrastus, 22, 31
Thousand and One Nights, The, 18, 50
Thurber, James, 32
Tieck, Ludwig, 12, 23
Todorov, Tzvetan, 3, 69
Tolkien, J.R.R., 34, 69
Toonder, Jan Gerhard, 7
Trask, Georgianne, 67
Trenkner, Sophie, 16, 68
Turgenev, Ivan, 24, 49
Twain, Mark, 33
Tynjanov, Jurij, 14, 70

Voltaire, 17, 22, 45
Vonnegut, Kurt, 45

Waidson, H.M., 23, 67
Walser, Robert, 32
Warren, Robert Penn, 60, 61
Welty, Eudora, 49, 66
West, Ray B., 66
Wilks, Ronald, 54
Wordsworth, William, 27, 28

Yeats, W.B., 8